Exploring *Vancouverism:*

The Political Culture of Canada's Lotus Land

by Howard Rotberg

CanadianValuesPress

Published by
CanadianValuesPress
Imprint of Mantua Books
Brantford, Ontario N3T 6J9
Vancouver B.C. V6K 4C4
Email: Mantua2003@Hotmail.com

National Library of Canada Cataloguing in Publication

Rotberg, Howard, 1951-
Exploring Vancouverism: The Political Culture of Canada's
Lotus Land

ISBN 978-0-9734065-1-1

1. Vancouver (B.C.)--Politics and government. 2. City planning—
British Columbia--Vancouver. 3. Vancouver (B.C.)--Intellectual
life. 4. Vancouver (B.C.)--Civilization. I. Title.

FC3847.394.R68 2008   971.1'33   C2008-906299-X

Front Cover
Richard is a "binner" – one of the hundreds of impoverished
Vancouverites who push shopping carts daily through parks and
back lanes. They search through garbage for recyclable cans and
bottles that they collect and sell to recycling depots and liquor
stores for 7 to 10 cents each.   Richard has a hard life, but was
very proud to pose for this photo.

Front and back cover photographs by the author.

This book is dedicated to my wife Penny Gurstein, not only a loving wife and mother, but also an astute observer, critic, and teacher of urban and community planning, and social justice issues.

Exploring *Vancouverism:*

The Political Culture of Canada's Lotus Land

Table of Contents

The charmed sunset linger'd low adown
In the red West: thro' mountain clefts the dale
Was seen far inland, and the yellow down
Border'd with palm, and many a winding vale
And meadow, set with slender galingale;
A land where all things always seem'd the same!
And round about the keel with faces pale,
Dark faces pale against that rosy flame,
The mild-eyed melancholy Lotos-eaters came.

Branches they bore of that enchanted stem,
Laden with flower and fruit, whereof they gave
To each, but whoso did receive of them,
And taste, to him the gushing of the wave
Far far away did seem to mourn and rave
On alien shores; and if his fellow spake,
His voice was thin, as voices from the grave;
And deep-asleep he seem'd, yet all awake,
And music in his ears his beating heart did make.

They sat them down upon the yellow sand,
Between the sun and moon upon the shore;
And sweet it was to dream of Fatherland,
Of child, and wife, and slave; but evermore
Most weary seem'd the sea, weary the oar,
Weary the wandering fields of barren foam.
Then some one said, "We will return no more";
And all at once they sang, "Our island home
Is far beyond the wave; we will no longer roam."

From "The Lotos Eaters", Alfred Tennyson

Preface:

Values in a Time of Financial Challenges

This book was completed just as a major economic decline has hit the global economy.

People with poor ethics convinced people with wants greater than their actual needs and wealth to borrow money that they could not reasonably pay back to the financial institutions whose greedy and high paid executives did not really care because they then bundled these financial products for sale to other institutions with executives whose salaries and bonuses far exceeded the type of prudence that bankers historically possessed. Politicians, professors and media who should all have been blowing the whistles were too caught up in benefitting from this system, obtaining funding, grants, advertising and the like.

Economic historians will no doubt analyze why all of this happened, as we inevitably deal with the repercussions for years to come.

But, surely, some of the important reasons that will be discussed are the culture of greed, the culture of consumerism, and the culture of debt that came to predominate in the United States, and elsewhere around the developed world. Canadian financial institutions were more prudent, and better regulated, and so they did not proceed down the same path of doomed residential mortgage lending. However, in our global economy, economies are so linked together that problems in the larger economies quickly affect the rest of the world.

What interests me, rather than the economics and the financial analysis of what went wrong, is how these cultures of greed, narcissism, consumerism and debt came to be so accepted.

Why are there so many people in their 70s and 80s living modestly at the same time they have bank balances in the millions of dollars? And why are there so many people from the following generations living in luxury when their bank balances are far exceeded by their debts?

The answer is *Culture;* or, put another way, *Ideology.*

The patterns of thought and the values people hold are what govern their choices of lifestyle and politics and economics and what essential choices they make in the way they live their lives.

And so, to analyze the politics and urban planning of any city requires a preliminary inquiry. It is that preliminary inquiry that is attempted by this book. That inquiry is to analyze the ideology and values, or lack of values, that exist in a certain area, as a precondition to understanding the municipal planning and political policies adopted in that area.

The great Canadian journalist and writer on all things political and economic in Canada, Peter C. Newman wrote a column in the October 11, 2008 issue of *The Globe & Mail*, in which he got to the essence of the matter:

"What we need is new gods, freshly minted mentors motivated by values as the source of their experience – instead of experience as the source of their values."

Accordingly, we explore Vancouver*ism:* The Political Culture of Canada's Lotus Land. In a time of economic and political challenges, it is key that, before we know where to go in the future, we understand where we are now, based on the ideologies and values that have predominated in the last few years. This book is my contribution to furthering that understanding.

Chapter 1: Introduction

The Ideology of the Lotos Eaters*

"The Best Place on Earth"

- New slogan of the Government of British Columbia, appearing on the new Olympic license plates, and various government publications

"It's one thing to like where you live. It's another to engage in the kind of self-satisfied back-patting that Vancouverites are often guilty of. Now to go with the commercials featuring people chirping the slogan, new B.C. license plates also bear the cringe-inducing The Best Place on Earth. If you have to say it, it's probably not true."

- *The Georgia Straight,* September 20, 2007

"11 out of 18"

- Vancouver's ranking among 18 Canadian cities in a study by the Canadian Institute for Advanced Research measuring satisfaction of residents with their lives. (Reported in *Vancouver Sun*, December 29, 2007)

It is perhaps trite to say that everyone sees life through their own set of values, experiences and desires. One of the joys of traveling is to experience new cultures, and hopefully, begin to learn a little about the prevailing thought-patterns in a new place, as well as the usual tourist attractions of the place.

---

* Tennyson's poem uses for the word "Lotus" the Greek version, "Lotos", and so I also use the Greek spelling when referring to Tennyson's poem, "The Lotos-Eaters".

Accordingly, as Vancouver gears up for the 2010 Olympic Winter Games, we are readying ourselves for the onslaught of tourists. And, as made clear above, we are attempting to tell such tourists that Vancouver, and in fact all of British Columbia, is the "best place on earth". Like *The Georgia Straight*, I think that such boasting is a little odd. More than a little odd, in fact, because where I grew up (small town Southern Ontario) we were taught that boasting about yourself was rude, and those who did boast were probably trying to mask some underlying insecurity.

When I first moved to Vancouver, I of course was impressed by the beauty of the natural setting, and the walkable neighbourhoods in the better sections of town, with proximity to all kinds of recreational opportunities, the fabulous Stanley Park, and the seawall and beaches. When it comes to parks, Vancouver does it very, very well.

And the restaurants! Such a diversity of quality restaurants of every type and ethnic fare, done with panache - and many are much more affordable than one would expect. The competition among Chinese, Japanese and Indian restaurants is intense, and the customers are the beneficiaries.

The weather is not too hot in the summer and not too cold in the winter. Especially in the summer, when you get many days with sunshine and 23 degrees, you feel, as you walk along the ocean, or rollerblade or bike along the seawall in Stanley Park, that this is paradise. Even in the winter, with the rain, donning a rain-jacket allows you to keep walking or bicycling, when most of the country is freezing and shoveling snow.

Vancouver has two of the finest swimming pools I have ever seen, one at Kits Beach and one at Second Beach in Stanley Park, both extremely long, with dedicated lanes for laps, filtered sea water, and vistas overlooking the ocean. It is not hard to understand why many visitors to Vancouver decide they would like to settle here.

But for some reason, I soon came to understand that Vancouver has a vastly different political and social culture than most other places in

Canada. The boasting about being the "best" co-existed with some dramatic problems, and, to be blunt, a shocking lack of care - about the way that certain sections of the population were given extraordinary benefits, and other sections of the population were at best being ignored, and at worst being taken advantage of by the various "vultures" in the community.

Here are some of the issues that we shall study in the following pages:

- there are legions of homeless, mentally ill, drug addicted folks scavenging through garbage bins;
- Vancouver is well behind every large city in Canada and most in the United States in terms of affordable housing inducement programs for the private sector and the non-profit sector
- Vancouver provides much more in the way of benefits without a means test to mature and wealthy property-owning people than it does to its young and its workforce
- Vancouver has a rather startling tolerance for criminals of every kind
- the so-called "Vancouver Model" of expensive downtown high rise one and two bedroom development evidences a blatant disregard for young families and Vancouver's workforce
- Vancouver's belief that it is a leader in environmentalism is not quite true
- the glorification of real estate developers with their leaky condos and investment dealers and promoters with their penny stocks is an insult to all those who have lost money due to willful fraud and/or negligence by the actors involved and by those who were supposedly regulating them
- Vancouver values esthetics and appearances far more than it values social justice
- Vancouver is making itself into a high-end resort without sufficient public debate about who is winning and who is losing under this change
- there is only a half-hearted attempt to police drug gangs and their extensive distribution networks, and the vast laundering of their money within seemingly legitimate business enterprises

So, why do Vancouver and British Columbia as a whole feel so strongly that they are the "best" and feel the need to constantly boast about it?

And why did I, when I moved here, see a very different picture than the one being promoted? Why do I shake my head when I see that the government of British Columbia publishes and distributes flashy little brochures with titles such as:

- *The Best Place on Earth for Sustainable, Livable Communities*
- *The Best Place on Earth for People in Need*
- *The Best Place on Earth for Patients*

To be sure, Vancouver has a stunning natural setting, ample parkland, proximity to recreational opportunities, great restaurants, and some nice buildings. Yet, even using the (mostly esthetic) standards by which Vancouver seems to judge itself as "the best place on earth", surely there are other cities that excel by those criteria. For example, San Francisco has the same geographical attributes, and moreover, has a stock of magnificent heritage buildings and museums and other cultural amenities that makes Vancouver's boasting seem puerile. The use of architectural detail and colour in San Francisco, quite frankly, makes Vancouver's uniformly beige, modernist Downtown, look flatly uninteresting in comparison.

The answer, of course, to why I see things so differently, is that I come from a different culture. In Canada, we are used to the fact that Quebec has a different culture from the rest of Canada, and we supposedly support something called *multiculturalism*. What we tend to diminish, at least in the mainstream media, is how these various cultures are based on different values, and different ways of seeing the world.

My background includes a degree in Cultural History; in my studies, I became very interested in the broad-based patterns of thought and values in any given society. Then I moved on to Law School and became a practicing Corporate and Real Estate Development Lawyer, in Ontario, for twenty years. But at the age of 45, I sold my practice, to put in use my skills in real estate development towards the development of affordable rental housing for the working poor and the moderate income workforce, who were having an increasingly difficult time finding appropriate accommodation due to the inflation of real estate and the lack of construction of new affordable rental housing. After a number of years as an affordable housing developer, and also as a writer, I moved to Vancouver, but when I got here, I arrived with a very different set of interests and values than what had become the norm in what I perceived to be a "Lotus Land".

In order to illustrate the way in which cultural values (or the lack thereof) underpin the wider political and social issues in Vancouver, I have used as a continuing metaphor, the great poem by Alfred Tennyson, called "The Lotos-Eaters". I would recommend that every High School literature program in Vancouver make the teaching of this poem compulsory.

I also, in Chapter 2, portray Vancouverism through the metaphor of a fable, adapted from "The Emperor's New Clothes". Hopefully, my techniques will shed some light on the inadequately understood cultural attitudes which seemingly allow for the continuation of some of the problems which I have summarized above, all the while gloating about how we are the "best".

Sometimes, we query how people cannot see the obvious, or, to put it another way, how can people disregard every fact that does not accord with their theories. Well, that is the effect of *Ideology.*

Once upon a time (when History was a compulsory subject in every year of High School), we seemed, as a society to have a better grasp of the role of ideology, in creating differing viewpoints. In the 20th century, it all seemed so easy to distinguish *liberals* from *conservatives, left* from *right,* and *progressives* from *reactionaries.* In the 21st century, the waters are far murkier.

Still, people cling to the familiar; in this case they cling to the familiar ideological categories of left versus right, etc., nothwithstanding that these categories are clearly passé. And the central division may be between those who, having partaken of the Lotos, deny the existence of Evil, and those who know what it is, and are resolved to do something about it. As Tennyson writes:

"What pleasure can we have to war with evil?"

And so, in a world inundated with political correctness and moral relativism, demanding only *tolerance* and not *action,* the Lotus eaters of Vancouver are the most politically correct of the politically correct: a diet of the Lotos, be it the actual fruit or leaves, or the cultural diet of the Lotos, leaves too many citizens uncaring of both past and future, good versus evil, all the while denying the reality of ideology itself.

Instead, as we shall see, the Lotos-Eaters have opted for a life of calm, a life of pleasure and a life of beauty. They decry the foibles of institutionalized religion, and with their yoga stretches and "lotus" positions, turn to a so-called spiritualism which is individualized and divorced from social action.

At the same time, the Lotos-Eaters pay little attention to the rampant crime around them, with the drug related crime, and the white collar crime in the investment and stock promoting community. Having decided not to "war with evil", they cannot even be bothered to "denounce" that evil, either.

When you are living a Lotus life of pleasure on a beach, the idea of planning for the future is often a low priority. That is why there is so little planning for how the next generation will afford housing; so little in the way of programs to induce the creation of affordable housing for low and even moderate income working people.

The Lotus folks of Vancouver hardly even plan for the possibility of the major earthquake that seismic experts estimate will hit Vancouver in the next 50 to 100 years. City Hall itself would not survive a moderate earthquake, but more worrying still is this fact, as reported in the May 14, 2008 *Vancouver Sun*: the B.C. government in 2004 identified more than 700 schools for seismic upgrades, yet, four years later, work has only begun on four of the 80 cases that were considered *urgent.* Neighbouring Seattle has already completed its school seismic retrofits, but "The Best Place on Earth" is too busy planning its Olympic parties, and promoting itself as a "green" city. It takes a special mentality to fail so dramatically at planning for the future.

This is the cultural context in which I view Vancouverism, and all of the cultural particularities and oddities of Vancouver. Of course, there are many cultures in Vancouver and hence many Vancouvers. What interests us in this book are some of the cultural undercurrents that make Vancouver unique, and its political choices understandable.

In Vancouver, most people I speak to have heard the term "Lotus Land" and know that is has something to do with the West Coast of Canada and the United States. Some know that it has something to do with drugs, some know that is has something to do with a laid-back type of lifestyle. But what is amazing to me is that so few have ever taken the 30 seconds necessary to google the term, and learn more than that. What is amazing to me is how so few care to know anything about the ideological framework of the society in which they reside. In this book, we shall discuss how the turning away from conventional religion in Vancouver has hastened a culture which is uncaring of contemplating things ideological. In a place where beauty and esthetics reign, self-praise and esthetic fulfillment have superceded an examination of values. If this book accomplishes anything, I hope it causes more people to actually read Tennyson's poem and contemplate the issues raised by it.

Vancouverism can be defined much more narrowly than I choose to define it. It can be defined narrowly as a program of urban planning that stresses the development of downtown areas with dense forms of housing – primarily slim skyscrapers rising out of a base of townhomes, calculated to give the streetscape a more friendly urban face than if the bases were simply parking garages, or such. It involves, as well, the granting of density bonuses to developers in return for the provision of public amenities.

A slightly wider definition would include the concept that downtowns ought to be *mostly* dense forms of housing, and less and less office buildings and commercial districts. Perhaps offices and commercial districts should be scattered among suburban nodes of development, to encourage less reliance on the automobile. Yet, if downtown districts welcome extreme densification, and suburban districts fight densification, then one can end up with commuters living downtown and commuting to the suburbs, with more and more of the formerly *urban* problems plaguing the suburbs, in a weird inversion of traditional patterns in the older cities of North America. Moreover, banishing the employers to suburban areas that are bereft of good public transit, is not a responsible act from the point of view of the working people who are also banished to these fringe car-oriented communities.

I am one of those who believe however that the narrow definitions of *Vancouverism* are inadequate to understand the culture in Vancouver. It is obvious to me, that the ideological glasses through which Vancouverites see their world, is a more complex matter than urban form downtown. And so, this book is my attempt to understand the effect of the cultural milieu of Vancouver, upon urban living and urban planning in this, Canada's Lotus Land.

After some time living here, I began to find some others who were starting to look at Vancouverism in a similar way. One of my favorites is the architectural critic Trevor Boddy. Here is one example of his astute observations:

"(T)here is a more serious addiction in this town, one that is talked about even less than crack or crank or smack. Gallons of it are consumed daily by our city planners, developers, designers and media managers, often after a session of hot yoga, or following a light meal of pickled lotus leaves, or even just sitting around swank coffee tables strewn with international accounts of our urban success.

They are drinking their own bathwater. What bugs me is that they are calling it champagne."

In essays such as "Vancouverism and its Discontents" (supra) and "Vancouverism vs. Lower Manhattanism: Shaping the High Density City", *ArchNewsNow.com*, September 20, 2005, Boddy has been one of the few Vancouverites to consistently place developments in Vancouver in the context of the wider world of architecture and city planning.   His frustration is that most Vancouverites, as he notes above, are "drinking their own bathwater" and "calling it champagne".

I fully understand the unwelcoming reaction that this enquiry is likely to stir up among the elites in this beautiful city.   In part, that is because my understanding of the term, *Ideology*, is one that is radical, by Vancouver standards.

When I first moved here, I had a discussion with a gentleman, who seemed quite bright, holds a Ph.D., and in all seriousness told me that he believes that Canadians do not, unlike Americans, hold an ideology.   The Americans, of course, under Bush, were "right wing", Christian fundamentalists, imperialists, racists, homophobic, etc., etc. But we Canadians, according to this fellow, were ideologically neutral.

I could not believe what I was hearing.   His views, of course, were the essence of "political correctness", a recent, fundamentally elitist form of ideology itself, which holds that if one is truly tolerant, fair, and pacifist, then one's own views are ideologically neutral - and only those who are too right wing and reactionary to be tolerant and fair have ideologies.

The fact that the idea that one is free of ideology, is in fact an ideology itself, does not occur to its proponents.   The fact that everyone sees life through a certain set of ideological assumptions of what is fair, what is good, and what is just, and that these assumptions are begging for constant re-examination, seems to be of little concern, especially to those I call, in Chapter 10, the "Starbucks Progressives".   Blaming the "other" for the world's problems, whether that other is America, or some more nuanced type of blame, is so often a way to close off discussion of those policies and viewpoints which are crying out for discussion.   In a city that denies ideology, except in the most anachronistic sense of Liberals versus NDP, organized labour versus business, and "progressive" members of City Council blocs versus pro-business City Council blocs, there seems to be less and less discussion of what is more and more important.

Accordingly, if nothing else, in this book, we shall strive to understand the ideological and cultural underpinning of urbanism and urban planning in Vancouver, and it is that wider picture that I choose to call *Vancouverism.* In Chapter 11, we shall discuss how the pretend "progressives" of Vancouverism are really reflecting a far different ideology, which I have named *Tolerism* – the excessive need to show tolerance of anything and everything, in some kind of revenge on those who respect religious values of Good versus Evil.

Having moved to Vancouver from Southern Ontario, a few years ago, I have both the advantages and disadvantages that come from being an "outsider". Certainly, one advantage is that I see that many of what are thought to be great ideological disputes by those in the thick of them here, are really just slight differences in what parts of the general consensus should be emphasized first, and what parts later. In other words, I have viewed in the past few years most all of the politicians here as tweedle-dums and tweedle-dees: In the words of the anonymously written nursery-rhyme:

> Tweedledum and Tweedledee
>   Agreed to have a battle;
> For Tweedledum said Tweedledee
>   Had spoiled his nice new rattle.
> Just then flew down a monstrous crow,
>   As black as a tar-barrel;
> Which frightened both the heroes so,
>   They quite forgot their quarrel.

Vancouver is one of the few big cities in Canada with party politics and without a ward system. Both facts act to preserve the status quo. As of the time of writing this (the summer of 2008, before the November 2008 elections), both Vision Vancouver and COPE (the Coalition of Progressive Electors) split the reformist vote, leaving the NPA (Non-Partisan Association) in power, where it has traditionally been – the party has picked 11 of Vancouver's 15 mayors since 1940. Worse still, there are no wards and no ward representation, leaving citizens without effective representation drawn from all components of the City. A so-called "non partisan" governing party is made up of councilors removed from the engagement of ward politics, and this has ill-served other priorities than those of the big developers and the rich property owners who see Vancouver as *their* Lotus Land. Insiders like bureaucrat/consultant Ken Dobell flit from the municipal administration to the provincial government and back again, having demonstrated their trustworthiness to preserve the status quo. Dobell, along with a partner, received a $300,000 commission to do an affordable housing study which, to be blunt, served to bury the techniques for municipal action behind policy recommendations which were mostly within the provincial jurisdiction. Query, whether City politicians got exactly the report that they wanted.

The NPA was established in 1937 to counteract the rise of the democratic socialist Commonwealth Co-operative Party. The NPA views itself as centre-right and draws its strongest support from the business community and Vancouver's established neighbourhoods on the west and south side. Its bizarrely ironic name stems from the ideological position that civic politics should *not* be driven by partisan, or party, politics.
This is yet another example of how Vancouverites have been fooled into believing that it is possible to be *post-ideological.* Of course, the NPA is ideological. This entire book shows what exact ideology the NPA has traditionally espoused.

How odd for a political party to call itself "non-partisan". A political party is by definition *partisan.* It is time that Vancouverites examine what the NPA's ideology is and what the ideology of Vancouverites should be. It is time to understand where we have been and where we are today, so that we know where we should be going in the future, and who is best qualified to lead us into that future. This book is a long exploration of just what ideology it is that has led us into such extremes of wealth and poverty and into what I term in Chapter 9 an outright "fraud on the young".

Lately the Coalition of Progressive Electors has shown signs of falling into the "loony left". Instead of concentrating on truly progressive policies for the people of Vancouver, they so often fall into empty symbolism. Wheelchair-bound former COPE councilor Tim Louis, otherwise a charming and bright man, goes about with a picture of Cuban revolutionary Che Guevera on the back of his wheelchair. The COPE website recently gave over its first page to promote a bizarre anti-Israel lecture by discredited former Israeli academic Ilan Pappe. COPE has to decide whether it is a world wide radical organization, taking on the liberal democracies like the U.S. or Israel, or is a municipal party, advancing the interests of working people. Right now, it is in danger of discrediting itself, leaving Vision Vancouver the only credible alternative to the partisan non-partisans.

Initial comments by COPE's sole sitting councilor, David Cadman, indicate that COPE may well back Vision's 2008 mayoral candidate Gregor Robertson, and avoid splitting the reformist vote.

If Robertson and Vision Vancouver unseat the NPA, we shall be interested to see if they can bring a fresh perspective unsullied by the regressive policies, based on the Lotus ideologies of the past. Look for COPE, down to one member of the current City Council, to gradually integrate into Vision (they were originally one party) or otherwise stay separate but agree on one mayoral candidate and agree to run an integrated slate of candidates, to allow a united opposition.

Vancouver is more than just a City, it is an idea. That idea is based in part on geography – the beauty of the mountains and the sea, the most moderate climate in Canada, where snow falls but a few days a winter.

In part, though, the idea of Vancouver, is what Alfred Tennyson took from Homer's *Odyssey.* The "Lotos Eaters" by Tennyson, is, for me, the central metaphor of Vancouver's culture. Citizens of Canada, the United States and beyond, who literally or figuratively have tired of their "roaming", have come to the shores of Lotos Land.

Whether they seek the "enchanted" lotos' stem and flower, or whether they seek only the clean sea air and the spectacular views and beaches, all seek to end their roaming, their struggles, and, in drinking in this Vancouverism, like the mariner of Odysseus, the pursuit of pleasure leads to "music in his ears his beating heart did make."

But, warns Tennyson, Lotos land is a place "where all things always *seem'd* the same" (my emphasis). Although the taste of the lotos and the vision of life it offers is seductive, the poem implies that the mariners may be deceiving themselves in succumbing to the hypnotic power of the lotos drug. Partaking of the lotos involves abandoning reality and living instead in a world of appearances, where everything "seems" to be but nothing actually is. If, as one mariner concludes in the poem, "We will return no more" to his homeland, is it merely out of addiction to the lotos plant?

Tennyson has the mariners state that they take "no pleasure" from a war against evil. If the measure of every act is the amount of pleasure derived therefrom, then surely the morality of the sojourn in the lotos land is undermined.

If Vancouver is just a lotus land, and just the geographic end of the line for those who would seek to roam, and for those in the rest of Canada who would seek to run away from their pasts, their families, and their memories, Vancouver is bound to fail at anything more worthy than the pursuit of pleasure and the pursuit of appearances. In Vancouver the appearances are so deceiving: a beautiful city full of creative people hides a massive institutionalized system of criminality, (primarily in the drug trade and in so-called "white-collar" crime like investment and stock fraud), a system of shoddy workmanship in housing construction (we shall deal later with the "leaky condo" fiasco), and a system of favours for the rich and powerful to the detriment of more modest income people - especially a system that protects the interests of wealthy older property owners to the detriment of the provision of affordable housing for younger people and our workforce.

To be sure, we must distinguish between the City of Vancouver and its suburbs and the rest of the province. The attitudes and ideologies change the further one gets away from downtown Vancouver. In addition we must distinguish the attitudes between native born Canadians and foreign born immigrants. In a *Vancouver Sun* article on December 15, 2007 commenting on the results of an Angus Reid survey on Canadian moral attitudes, Douglas Todd states:

"New immigrants are increasing the proportion of Canadians who are conservative about what is right and wrong – especially about family values and sex – and nowhere is that more true than in B.C."

This suggests that in the future, continued large immigration from Asia may start to erode some of the fundamental Lotus-type values described in this book. But, at present, the ideology of Vancouver itself, as opposed to the suburbs, is symptomatic of the values of the Lotos Eaters. It remains to be seen whether the second and third generations of new immigrants will manifest attitudes closer to their parents or closer to the dominant Lotus Land culture.

For younger people, probably the main thing about Vancouverism is the high (some might say "*ridiculous*") real estate prices. The Real Estate Board of Greater Vancouver divides its statistics between properties on the West side of the city and those on the East side of the city, and between detached houses and condo apartments. It publishes monthly figures for the yearly change in the "benchmark" price for those categories.

The *benchmark* price is the total value of all the properties divided by the number of properties.

(The *median* home price, on the other hand, is the threshold which divides the real estate market into two equal halves, in reference to pricing. One half of all homes in the market were sold at a price above the median home price, while the other half were sold below that price.)

As of February, 2008, the *benchmark* price of a resale condominium apartment on the West side of Vancouver reached $498,392, an increase from the year before of 14%. For the East side, the benchmark price of a resale condo apartment reached $329,376, up an even larger 18.1% from February, 2007.

The benchmark price for a detached house on the West side of Vancouver reached $1.45 million and just below $686,000 on the East side. A common topic at cocktail parties is whether this is a "bubble" ready to burst, as has happened in so many American markets recently, or is Vancouver a special micro-real estate market with endless demand for the privilege of living in the "Best Place on Earth".

As we shall see later in this study, the eye-popping prices and the double digit increases have created a speculation in condo units and a real perversion of priorities in the lives of those buying shelter in such a market. Such increases will not last (and recent forecasts in the fall of 2008 call for a 10% fallback in prices), but the orgy of construction and development in the first decade of the 21st century has left an indelible stamp on Vancouver. We shall examine in more detail, in Chapter 4, just how the culture surrounding housing has become a key component of Vancouverism.

The question for Vancouver's residents is: what more than beauty, high real estate values, and drugs does Vancouver stand for? Is Vancouver all about appearances, and nothing more than appearances? The next chapter starts our exploration of this very question.

If Vancouver's culture is based on the Lotos-Eaters, we may therefore have more in common with the American west coast cities, than we do with the rest of Canada.   Vancouver has extremes of wealth and poverty, and there is a growing differential between the "propertied" classes and those who cannot afford the million dollar houses. Our middle class is collapsing, because it takes an income of hundreds of thousands of dollars a year to afford nice housing here.   I am not sure if this central fact has really been clearly understood.

In Chapter 5, and other chapters, we shall explore more deeply the ideological aspects of the Lotos.

But as you, the reader, join me in my exploration of Vancouverism, I ask that you consider two central questions:

Can a culture valuing primarily the esthetic and the lotus, and viewing the world through the prism of pleasure-seeking narcissism, *ever* develop a local politics infused with morality and social justice?

And, do enough people really care?

Chapter 2

The Emperor's New City: Not a Fairy Tale

It was quite an embarrassing episode, that problem with the new clothes. He had paid so much for the clothes, and believed the salesmen who said that not only were they made of the most beautiful cloth, but this cloth was only visible to those who were not too stupid to see it.

He had sent his top two bureaucrats to check it out, and they said the cloth was beautiful, not wanting to admit that they might be stupid and not be able to see it. So what was an emperor to do? He could not very well admit that he could not see the clothes, so he paraded through the town wearing no clothes, and none of the townspeople wanted to admit that they were too stupid to see this fine cloth, so no one said anything, until a small child said, "But he has nothing on!"

The Emperor was so embarrassed he did not leave his castle for months. Finally, his most trusted bureaucrat came to him, and said, "Your majesty, we cannot change what has happened here. Why don't you start fresh as Emperor of a new city? I know just the place - the most beautiful, the most successful, the most livable city in all the world … situated between the mountains and the sea. Most of what was ugly has now been demolished, and replaced with the most beautiful buildings, populated by the most beautiful people. Your majesty will be very happy there."

And that is the story of how the Emperor came to dwell in New City. He consulted one of the best of the demi-gods of the place (such demi-gods being called "Real Estate Agents"), and purchased not his usual type of castle, but a two-storey "penthouse" castle in a shiny tower in the sky, facing the sea and the sacred place called The Park.

He hired some of the best bureaucrats to help him rule this new city. They explained that Traditional Religions had been banished in New City, in favour of "New Cityism" – a worship of the image of New

City as the finest and most beautiful city in the land. Now the culture worshiped beautiful houses, beautiful views, interior and exterior design, the mountains and the ocean, environmentalism, fitness, fine wines and fine marijuana. Then they told him that the new religious belief of New Cityism was in large part based on something called "Anti-comparisonism".

His advisors explained to him that this "Anti-comparisonism" meant that he must never look east beyond the mountains to the backwards place called "Rest of the Country", because the only ideas that were important and modern emanated from New City.
Most of all he was warned against ever looking south to the land with the Large Bush, because everything bad in life emanated from the land of the Large Bush, and everything great about New City was how it differed from the land of the Large Bush and the Rest of the Country. He was warned that there was no better policy to maintain the status quo in New City than deflect the attention of the citizens from any apparent problem - by pointing out how much better New City and its rulers are when compared to those in the Land of the Large Bush.

His bureaucrats warned him: "Your majesty, remember that your Kingdom depends on this: Never, never depart from our mantra that 'New City is the best, New City is the most beautiful.' "

The Emperor decided to tour New City from end to end, and this is what he saw:

Indeed the population of New City was disproportionately middle-aged, highly educated people who were millionaires by virtue of the astounding value of their houses. Many of them did not work in New City at all, some being early retired due to their wealth, and some working in far off places. In fact so many flew airplanes because of their work, that they made certain that the greatest priority for rapid transit was not to ease the commute of the working people who could only afford housing in the Suburbs yet worked in New City, but to allow the wealthy denizens of New City to effortlessly get to the Airport on their way to exotic vacations and their work elsewhere.

The whole downtown had been redeveloped for some reason as high-rise condos with one or possibly two bedrooms. This child-free zone was touted as New City's success story. The young people of New City could not really afford to have children, so they had to choose a childless existence in the Beautiful Downtown, or be banished to the far suburbs where family housing was more affordable. Apparently some of the top bureaucrats responsible for this model of redevelopment of the most expensive property in the entire Land had no children themselves and their vision was welcomed by a population not daring to challenge the experts. They did not want to appear *stupid.*

Surely it would be *stupid* to ask why all the policies were geared to providing millions of square feet of new condo towers every year, and *no* square feet of new modest rental apartments every year. Surely the god called The Market had dictated this, and no one should attempt to constrain his omnipotence and knowledge of what was best for New City.

No one asked whether there were policy changes that might be implemented to induce private sector developers to produce affordable rental housing. No one wanted to ask such a *stupid* question.

Then the Emperor noticed that the Municipal Planners who were supposed to regulate the Big Developers had a tendency after a few years to leave his employ and go to work for more money for the Big Developers. He wondered if this might be a problem, but everyone assured him this was normal.

The child-less and the empty-nesters were paying more and more for less and less, in the way of housing. Apparently, the people also worshipped hardwood and granite.

It was clear that lower and middle income "working people" making under the $120,000 per year family income necessary to buy a modest home in New City, could only reside in New City if some new affordable rental housing would be built. Apparently, New City had abolished Affordable Rental Housing. What little of it was left, was being bought by investors. The demi-god Real Estate Agents were selling investors rental buildings that carried the ridiculously low returns of a 3.75% "cap rate". They then demonstrated their divine-given skills by counseling the investors that they could then evict the lower income tenants, make some superficial renovations, and re-rent at inflated prices.

Unlike in the country of the Large Bush, and in the Rest of the Country, there was no effort at all to provide financial inducements to encourage the construction of *new* rental buildings. Apparently no one in New City cared that these tenants would be forced to move to the place called the Suburbs, and become part of the cursed Sprawlism. The citizens of New City strutted their commitment to Environmentalism and densification, even as they banished the lower and middle income working classes to the Suburbs -and then looked down on them for their stupid use of cars and highways and bridges to get to their jobs in New City

No one noticed that with such a critical shortage of rental buildings, the landlords did not have to house the less than desirable tenants, and could with a paint job and new flooring get middle income tenants instead. The previous tenants, then dropped "out the bottom" of this new rental system and they became Homeless.

No one was allowed to look at the dozens of successful programs to induce the private sector away from building only condos and into affordable rental housing that were working so well in the Rest of the Country and in the Land of the Large Bush. Instead, the population of New City decided that having no new Rental Housing was best for New City, so that all future neighbours would be high income, highly educated people, and not threaten what was really important in New City – the god called Property Values.

Of course, agreed the wealthy homeowners, these inducement programs cost money, and there is a limit to how many tax increases can be passed on to the public, even a very wealthy public. But no one asked if the nearly $1 billion spent on a new Convention Centre might have been better spent on inducements to create affordable housing. No one asked where all the waiters and waitresses working in the new Convention Centre would live, since their salaries would be too low to live in New City.

The High Priest of the Kingdom utilized his folksy charm to advocate something trendy sounding called "EcoDensity". As far as the Emperor could see, this was a way for developers to make more money on more tall condo buildings. The developers were being encouraged to provide environmental upgrades and also public "amenities" as part of their developments. This was a way to make the new residents of these towers, the young people paying $375,000 for a small one-bedroom, to pay the cost of these features through higher purchase prices.   More importantly it was a way for the existing residents to avoid paying for new public amenities, and the new environmentalism, through increased property taxes. He could see that this was another way to make the moderate income people pay more and the rich less.   Then, with the resulting high costs of new housing (made even more expensive by "green" features for the environment), the property values of the existing residents kept going up to keep pace with new construction. The Emperor realized what a good system this was for the existing property owners.

He was a little concerned that so many of the new condo towers seemed to develop major construction problems after a few years. So many seemed to be leaking water. He wasn't sure if this was because the developers and architects and engineers didn't know how to build better buildings, or because they didn't much care if their buildings were built properly. The Emperor was assured that this could not be a real problem because property values were still going up.

Even the University in New City used its excess land to build million dollar townhouses and $600,000 two-bedroom condos. Surrounding its students with upper income housing, exquisite ample parkland and pristine (clothing-optional) beaches was seen as instilling the right values in the future ruling class of New City.

The Emperor came to understand the role of marijuana and alcohol – it was to keep the young intoxicated enough so that they would not think too hard about how New City was so unwelcoming to them as to housing and secure employment.   And if they became too depressed about their prospects, then there were always the harder drugs.

New City closed many of the institutional beds for the mentally ill, and instead rounded them and the very poor, the addicted, and all the others who could not live their lives according to the standards of New Cityism (and could not or would not leave for the Suburbs) into a four square block section. The Emperor thought that this was quite a good idea, because if there were no institutions left to house them, at least they could access helping services, safe injection sites and the like, rather than hiding in parks and under bridges in the better neighbourhoods of New City.   The only problem was the Real Estate Agents and the Developers were running out of other land to develop and had their eyes on cheap land in this "theme park for the mentally ill and the addicted".

Accordingly, the Real Estate Developers and the Politicians began to look anew at the remaining 244 acres of what had been a large institution for the mentally ill in a suburb of Vancouver, but was severely downsized to get the mentally ill back into the "community". Unfortunately, this assumed that the "community" would allow and encourage the construction of supportive housing in their neighbourhoods, which turned out not to be the case.   So it was realized that instead of taxing the rich property owners of Greater Vancouver an amount sufficient to renovate and upgrade that facility, much of the land could then be sold to developers at the current inflated rates.   Then there would be no cost to the existing property owners, because the developers would then just pass the costs on to the owners of these new condos to be built surrounding the asylum for the mentally ill.   These new owners, young people and new immigrants would then serve the needs of the existing wealthy in a creative way: first, the cost of upgrading the psychiatric facility would be passed along to these new owners of condos, creating ever increasing prices, since the price of the condos would reflect the high price the Province would get for the land;   second, the higher price of the new condos would in turn increase the market values of existing houses, thus ensuring that the existing property owners would not only *not* have to pay for the facilities needed, but that they would indirectly *benefit* from the higher price of real estate that these young people and new immigrants would have to pay; and third, these new condo towers that would surround the rehabilitated psychiatric institution would act as the perfect buffer so that the wealthy would no longer have to see the mentally ill, and the existing mentally ill could be shipped away from the upscale neighbourhoods of New City.   A perfect New City solution, if the Province and the suburbs would just accept the plan.

The religious beliefs of New Cityism, concentrating on the belief in New City's success and the worship of its beauty, meant that it was improper to spend money on Affordable Housing, or to help the underclass in this "theme park".   The Emperor understood, as he looked around New City, that this was all a religious imperative.   And so, he understood, that the most important use of tax money was to create great Convention Centres and Luxury Hotels for those who chose to come and worship in New City as they conducted conventions, business or personal touring.   Next, he understood the need to spend billions to host the Great Sporting Event.

The Great Sporting Event was the emblem of all that was important with New Cityism.   Impressing the world with the beauty and accomplishments of New City was of course the central theme of everything that New Cityism stood for.   No expense was too great, no cost overrun too embarrassing to create the supreme religious event for New Cityism.   Never mind that the Great Sporting Event was to take place when the construction costs of labour and materials were at record levels, and shortages of same would inevitably result in cost overruns.   It was not important.   Never mind that housing for the athletes was first "sold" to the people as expanding the supply of affordable housing. Blatant reduction of the affordable components of such housing would surely be accepted as so few in New City really wanted the affordable housing and its occupants anyway.

What to do with all the Homeless, the mentally ill, the addicted and the panhandlers, who would surely harm the very fundamental image of New Cityism during the Great Sporting Event?   The High Priest of

New City formulated a program, "Project Civil City" to reduce the problems by 50% by the time of the Great Sporting Event. The Emperor thought this was probably just a temporary program for the duration of the Great Sporting Event. He guessed that, upon its conclusion, these homeless and mentally ill, would be released back on the street from wherever they were to be put for the duration of the Event.

The Emperor began to understand that New City accepted only certain kinds of disabled people. Physical disabilities or aged based disabilities were acceptable, but not mental disabilities. Anyone who suffered from mental, as opposed to physical disability, was excluded by the combination of lack of treatment, lack of supportive housing, and lack of new lower rent affordable housing – such affordable rental housing being necessary for those whose mental disabilities allowed them to live independently but prevented them from earning high enough wages to become property owners in New City.

The Emperor learned quickly. One neighbourhood of fine homes dealt quickly with an attempt to put in smaller more affordable homes – the homes were torched before they could be finished.

In New Cityism, learned the Emperor, the promotion of the inequities of the status quo hid behind concern for "seniors". There was of course no concern for "juniors" or how young people would ever afford housing, unless they had wealthy parents. Even the Housing Strategy only pretended to be concerned for them, by upping the limit for waiver of Property Transfer Tax to $375,000, for first time buyers. This of course was really not a policy to expand affordable housing, but was really a benefit to big developers to help them sell more one-bedroom condos to upper-middle class younger people.

He learned that New Cityism had complicated programs to help the rich, property owning class, even as it pretended there was no money to help build affordable rental housing for the young members of the working class. The Emperor learned of a program that allowed seniors, *without a means test*, to avoid paying property taxes, and defer the taxes until sale of their homes or death at a low interest rate of 4%.

The new Housing Strategy even dropped the minimum age for this benefit to 55. The Emperor was puzzled at why young people had "bought into" supporting this program that effectively put more money in the pockets of wealthy seniors owning million dollar homes, without any necessity of proving they needed such help. Then he realized that the priests of New Cityism had created a mantra called "aging in place" and no matter that the place was a multi-million dollar ocean-view home, young people, properly educated, knew that it was important to support that right, rather than make these unfortunate millionaires move to $600,000 condos and upset their lives.

He learned that additional money was going as Homeowner's Grants to help the "landed class" with the costs of property taxes. These poorer citizens of New City, who could only afford $900,000 homes rather than multimillion dollar homes were getting a grant from the public coffers to help them in the difficult years until their homes, too, inflated to millions of dollars. In 2008, the maximum value of homes for which assistance was available was raised to $1,050,000.

The Emperor gradually learned that New Cityism was meant to protect the interests of those with property. He noted that the doctrine of "anti-comparisonism" meant that no one in New City even realized that the property taxes on a million dollar house in New City were only about 60% of the property taxes on a similarly priced house in a similarly sized city in the Rest of the Country. Knowledge of this might cause some pressure to redistribute the income of the wealthy citizens of New City, and persuade them that indeed there was a municipal source of revenue that could go to affordable housing. Anti-comparisonism also meant that few realized how out of wack was the ratio of property taxes for business assessed property compared to residential assessed property. While, in the Rest of the Country, the ratio was close to 1:1, in New City, businesses paid almost six times the property taxes as similarly priced residential properties. Small business owners, including those in rented space, where the property taxes are passed on to the tenant, were paying so much property tax that they were often having to work seven days a week themselves just to make ends meet.

The Emperor saw that the doctrine of anti-comparisonism was so effective in preventing his subjects from demanding change. He let it be known that the reason property values were so high in New City was because of the influx of the People of the Far East, and therefore the problems were essentially insoluble. This approach worked in tandem with the philosophy of Blame the Other. Had his subjects looked to the south or to the east, they would have seen that every large, successful city in the Rest of the Country and in the Land of the Large Bush, was struggling with very similar inflation of property values, but they, as opposed to New City, were implementing policies to provide affordable rental housing to lower income working people. The Emperor came to a real appreciation as to how the doctrine of Anti-Comparisonism helped achieve social peace and a docile lower class.

New City and the Lord of Provincialism decided to issue special automobile license plates the sale of which would help fund the Great Sporting Event. The Emperor chose a special slogan for the top of the license plate: "The Best Place on Earth". The Lord of Provincialism decided to make this the slogan for all his government departments, for surely there could be no better place in the entire earth.

Then the Emperor discovered a neat way to stay in power and thwart any opposition from people who might view New City differently. He declared that he and his Council were going to govern, not by partisan politics, but by non-partisan politics; therefore, there was no need to challenge the policies, because they were not policies, not partisan, not political at all. He decided to call his fellow Councilors members of the NPPPP – the Non-Political Party political party.

So, as the Emperor toured his new domain, he felt good. He felt that he now understood the principles of New Cityism, and he was prepared to lead. And indeed for the next few years the Emperor was widely feted and loved for his wholehearted adoption of New Cityism.

Finally came the opening ceremonies for the Great Sporting Event in 2010. The whole world was watching New City, basking in its success at funding and staging this wonderful event, and showing off its beauty to the world. The Emperor was invited to speak. Before he started, a beautiful young 10 year old girl was chosen to bring to him on the stage a bouquet of flowers. The Emperor beamed as she handed him the flowers. With the microphone on, he asked the child, "so my dear, what do you think of New City now?"

The child paused for a second, and then said, "It's nice, *but where will I live?*"

This was whispered from person to person in the crowd, until everyone was shouting, "yes, but where shall she live?" The shouting kept getting louder and louder. Then they starting clapping their hands and stomping their feet, all the while shouting, "where shall she live?", while the little girl started to cry.

The Emperor heard the shouts, but he turned away from the crowd and looked at the beautiful new athletic buildings. He smiled at the Big Name architects who were sharing the stage with him. He tried not to hear the crowd, instead concentrating on all that was good and beautiful in New City.

Chapter 3

Ellison Wonderland: Narcissism in Vancouverism

Humpty Dumpty and Alice:

"**Humpty Dumpty:** When I use a word, it means just what I choose it to mean - neither more nor less.
Alice: The question is, whether you can make words mean so many different things.
Humpty Dumpty: The question is: which is to be master - that's all."

Lewis Carroll, *Alice in Wonderland*

"And music in his ears his beating heart did make."

Alfred Tennyson, "The Lotos Eaters"

In this chapter, we consider the story of Vancouver teacher Tom Ellison and his serial sexual abuse and inappropriate behaviour with students of his outdoor education program at Prince of Wales High School in a high income area of Vancouver. The story was tragic for all involved, and, while Ellison was finally convicted criminally many years after the abuse, the story has not ended. To be sure, the subjects of his abuse will live with the emotional effects always, and Mr. Ellison's disgrace is permanent.   But what appears to have been missed in this whole sad saga, is how very *Vancouver* is the tale; and more specifically how the story is all about the psychological condition of *narcissism*; and what the story tells us about narcissism as a component part of *Vancouverism.*

First some background about the condition of narcissism:

According to Israeli writer Sam Vaknin,

"Pathological narcissism is a life-long pattern of traits and behaviours which signify infatuation and obsession with one's self to the exclusion of all others and the egotistic and ruthless pursuit of one's gratification, dominance and ambition."

The narcissist is basically insecure, and obsesses about himself, but the more obsessive he is about the object of his affection (himself), the less he likes what he sees.

Vaknin says that the symptoms of narcissism are as follows:

- "Feels grandiose and self-important (e.g., exaggerates accomplishments, talents, *skills, contacts, and personality traits to the point of lying, demands* to be recognized as superior without commensurate achievements);

- Is *obsessed* with fantasies of unlimited success, *fame, fearsome* power or *omnipotence, unequalled* brilliance *(the cerebral narcissist), bodily* beauty *or sexual performance (the somatic narcissist)*, or ideal, *everlasting, all-conquering* love *or passion*;

- Firmly convinced that he or she is unique and, being special, can only be understood by, *should only be treated by*, or associate with, other special or unique, or high-status people (or institutions);

- Requires excessive admiration, *adulation, attention and affirmation – or, failing that, wishes to be feared and to be notorious (Narcissistic Supply)*;

- Feels entitled. *Demands automatic and full compliance* with his or her unreasonable expectations for special and *favourable priority* treatment;

- Is "interpersonally exploitative", i.e., *uses* others to achieve his or her own ends;

- *Devoid* of empathy. Is *unable* or unwilling to identify with, *acknowledge, or accept* the feelings, needs, *preferences, priorities, and choices* of others;

- Constantly envious of others *and seeks to hurt or destroy the objects of his or her frustration. Suffers from persecutory (paranoid) delusions as he or she* believes that they feel the same about him or her *and are likely to act similarly*;

- Behaves arrogantly and haughtily. *Feels superior, omnipotent, omniscient, invincible, immune, "above the law", and omnipresent (magical thinking). Rages when frustrated, contradicted, or confronted* by people he or she considers inferior to him or her and unworthy."

  - Sam Vaknin, "What is Pathological Narcissism?", http://samvak.tripod.com/npdglance.html

Now, let us return to the story of Tom Ellison, and what I call, "Ellison Wonderland". During the 1970s and '80s, Ellison, a tall, handsome single man, then in his 30s, ran a program called Quest, at Prince of Wales High School. Selected students spent a semester foregoing the classroom in favour of canoeing, hiking, skiing, rock climbing and biking.

Jane Green, was one of the students in the Quest program, and after Ellison's criminal trial wrote a compelling piece called "Ellison's Quest", in the May, 2007 issue of *Vancouver Magazine*. She describes her teacher:

"Tom was the coolest teacher ever, a charismatic "rebel' full of anti-capitalist rants and hippie ideals who loved the outdoors and instantly made you long for his attention and approval.

"Between trips, we stayed in the Questroom, isolated from the rest of the school. We were earning credits towards English and Social Studies, but I don't remember any textbooks. Instead, the teachers lectured us on Quest ideology—'peace, love, and save the whales', as we used to say. Questors were to shun drugs and alcohol, maximize physical fitness, and love and preserve nature.

"There were no desks; we sat on the floor, acolytes, while the teachers held forth. Tom gave long rambling lectures. A favourite topic was ex-Questors he liked: 'classics,' he called them. Sometimes he grew indignant at another type of ex-Questor, the ones who'd betrayed him. One time he became angry because he had seen an ex-Questor wearing a fur coat. He felt she was thumbing her nose at his values. We joined in his outrage, promised ourselves we'd never betray Tom. 'It was cult-like in the sense that we were taught that what happened within those four walls was the truth,' (former student) Laura recalls. 'No one wanted to be the one to bring that down.'

"Each school day began with a workout in the Questroom, across from the principal's office. When we did Simon Says to warm up, Tom would have us touch our breasts, often teasing this or that girl about her development. When we did stretching, he'd walk around and make lewd comments about what he could see, and we'd giggle nervously."

Tom Ellison had a sailboat, to which he invited his favorite students. Tom's favorites not only got to visit on his boat, but their pictures were posted in the classroom. Although Ellison's sexual abuse of his students occurred in the '70s and '80s, it wasn't until a chance meeting of two abused female students in 1992 led to formal complaints. Both of the students realized that their abuse by this "coolest teacher ever" was the source of years of depression and emotional illness. Another two students then gave complaints and the police started an investigation, but by 1995, decided to shelve it for lack of sufficient evidence.

It wasn't until the year 2000 that another ex-Quester named Bridget Ross, who had a thirteen year relationship with Ellison, decided to complain, and with it, gave the names of some 30 other students she suspected of having been abused. It wasn't until 2004 that the police decided to charge Ellison with six counts of gross indecency and two counts of indecent assault. By the summer of 2006, the number of complainants had grown to twelve, and the charges had increased to twelve counts of gross indecency and four counts of indecent assault.

Green, who attended the trial, recalls how the Crown Attorney described "how girls we knew used to get on their bikes and pedal around town to hook up with Tom. His seduction technique was calculated and highly effective. It began with the sexualization of the classroom, singling out girls, telling them how special they were, slow dancing with them ... at after-school parties in the Questroom. Next came invitations to his boat. On sailing trips there would be talk of being a doer, of following your heart. There would be skinny-dipping and massages. A girl would find herself alone on the boat with Tom. His sure-fire move was to massage a girl's back, then whisper in her ear, 'Turn over.' The frontal massage would progress to a full-on encounter."

The pain for victims of Ellison's abuse was exacerbated, because there were in fact complaints that were dismissed by school administrators. Says Jane Green, "My own mother was approached by a school trustee (and family friend) who asked if there was truth to the rumours of sex between students and teachers in Quest. If ever there was an open secret on the west side of Vancouver, it was Tom Ellison's relationships with 'his girls.' And the sexualization of the program went well beyond Tom. Another teacher, Dean Hull, ended up in a long-term relationship with a Prince of Wales girl. Quest teacher Stan Callegari went on to marry one of his former students."

So Tom Ellison, narcissist *par excellence*, demanded adulation from the students in his "special" program, demanded and felt entitled to sexual services from 15 year olds, exploited them, felt no empathy or understanding about the lifetime of mental anguish and self-blame he was creating for these girls, raged against those who betrayed him, and excused everything because he was, after all, an environmentalist in his teaching, and after resigning his teaching position, became an "eco-tour" guide.

Ellison could have pled guilty to the charges, but instead he put his victims through a two week trial, where his lawyer argued that what he did was not a criminal offence at the *time he did it,* and then subjected the complainants to the usual indignities of cross-examination. The Judge could have taken that into consideration in the sentencing, along with the horrible impact of his crimes on his victims. In fact, one of the victims allegedly suffered a further nervous breakdown during the trial. But the Judge saw other factors as more important.

The Crown Attorney asked for a sentence of three to five years in jail. The Judge, however, refused to sentence Ellison to *any* jail time, instead giving him a sentence of "house arrest", for two years less a day, followed by one year of probation. The Judge called Ellison's acts "unforgivable" and a "monstrous breach of trust," but argued he had since turned his life around and didn't deserve jail.

And how had Ellison turned his life around, in order to avoid jail time for this "monstrous breach of trust"? Was he caring for the sick and homeless, was he devoting his life to charity and public service?

No, actually, he was running an eco-tourism business. Tom Ellison was extremely fortunate that Ellison Wonderland was in the one place in Canada that puts "eco-tourism" up so high on a pedestal that a man can avoid jail for sexually abusing his young students, and snicker at them as they relive their abuse on the witness stand.

The law of sentencing is actually supposed to take four factors into consideration: protection of the public, deterrence, rehabilitation and denunciation. The last factor, "denunciation" is something of a deterrence addressed to the rest of society. The Court, in a case where there is "monstrous", "unforgivable" behaviour should take into account in sentencing the need to *denounce* the conduct so strongly by use of jail time, so that society and the culture will understand that this conduct is most reprehensible. Failure to give Ellison jail time, softens the denunciation factor.

Probably, there is a confusion in liberal society between denunciation and vengeance. They are not related at all. There is no need to take vengeance on the criminal, but if we fail to leave the impression that "monstrous" behaviour is worthy of jail time, then are we really denouncing it? As usual, actions speak louder than words.

Ellison Wonderland, that sexual playground of a narcissistic outdoor education teacher, took place in one of the wealthiest areas of one of Canada's wealthiest cities. There was no secret about what was happening there. The daughters of wealthy lawyers, doctors and businessman, were being abused. More than 20 years later, the perpetrator is convicted, but escapes jail, because he quit teaching to run an eco-tourism business.

Ellison Wonderland is all about a narcissistic environmentalist. Old fashioned values like taking responsibility for your conduct pale in the face of West Coast values of boating and environmentalism.

Vancouverism understands and sympathizes with one of its own.

Vancouverism obsesses about how admired it is by the rest of the world. Whenever any organization does a study to show that Vancouver is one of the most "livable", "beautiful" or otherwise successful cities, according to this or that criterion, that makes front page news, here in Vancouver. It is like actress Sally Field clutching her new Oscar, in 1985, and crying out, "You like me, right now you really like me."

It is as if Vancouver, without the history of cities like Paris, London and Rome, and even without the history of Toronto, Montreal and most of the cities back east, feels insecure about its image as a "global city". There is still an anxiety that the "real" Vancouver, a rough and ready home to forestry, mining, stock manipulation, and hippies, will somehow be found under the veneer of beautiful buildings and upscale everything.

So Vancouver obsesses about itself and its titles as "best of", "most livable", etc. Loving itself and the reflection of the new condo towers in the waters of Burrard Inlet and False Creek, Vancouver, like the Emperor in Chapter 2, refuses to empathize with the rest of Canada, and even with its own working people, its own young, and anyone who lives outside the boundaries of its high priced real estate.

Vancouverites feel an excessive need to have urban planners from U.S. cities with tired downtowns, come and praise our vital downtown of expensive condos.   Lance Berelowitz's well received 2005 treatise on Vancouver was, of course, called *Dream City: Vancouver and the Global Imagination.* Obsessed about how we are viewed globally, we have neglected to think about how we are viewed by our own young and our own working people.   That is why we use our money to host the Olympics, rather than house our needy and our lower income workers.

As Susan Schwartz, writing on the topic of modesty for CanWest News Service on January 7, 2008, stated:

"To define yourself based on what other people think of you is a dangerous practice. You risk losing your own centre, for one, so that you're not quite sure anymore what you think."

Another problem with an insecure person overcoming his insecurity by falling in love with his own self-image is that there is very often a discrepancy between the reality and the image.   Tom Ellison fell in love with his image as the anti-establishment, environmentalist, hip, outdoorsman teaching his charges something the classroom couldn't teach – the natural, anti-corporate world of the outdoors, the sea, the mountains, and the sensual life.   The main problem is the reality is that he was mainly a pervert, breaching society's implicit contract with those to whom it entrusts its young – the contract of teaching, not using and abusing.

In a sense, Vancouver's self-love has done the same thing. Falling in love with its self-image as the global city, with the best quality of life, attracting the rich and famous to its downtown of expensive child-free condo towers, masked the reality of a city council and a planning staff breaching its duty to its citizens, young and old, to create a livable city, livable for *all* its residents.

We are not that different from other cities.   But those other cities are starting to "get it".   Toronto can no longer promote the myth that it is two cities, one an anti-sprawl Jane Jacobs-approved city of neighbourhoods in the "416" area code, and the other a sprawling car-oriented "905" area code of suburbs like Mississauga, Thornhill, Richmond Hill, Markham, Pickering, Ajax, etc.

Even Paris, the great legendary city of Europe was rudely brought to its senses, when rioting bands of North African Muslim youth in the ghettoized downscale high-rise banlieues (suburbs), starting in Clichy-sous-Bois, made the statement that they too deserved to be part of one of the supposedly greatest cities on earth.   The same can be said of every great city: there is the image of the culturally rich, architecturally splendid parts of the city, and then there is the reality of the deficient housing in the poor ghettos, whether those are in the central city or the suburbs.   In a sense, American cities, having their poorest citizens in their downtown areas, and most visible, are more likely to take steps towards creating affordable rental housing and social housing, because the problem is front and centre.   The "Vancouver model" is to dress up your highest profile neighbourhoods downtown, removing the issue of affordability from the mainstream, and diffusing the problem across many suburbs outside the Vancouver boundary.

So the image of Vancouver, as being a city only within its actual city limits, is a myth, a product of narcissistic self-love.   The reality is that Downtown Vancouver has been transformed into upscale one and two bedroom condos, many owned by people who only live in them part-time, others owned by corporations and investors, none serving the real needs of a city with young people and working people. Hence the real city now includes Surrey, Richmond, North Vancouver, Delta and all the other cities of the Fraser Valley that now are a *de facto* part of Metropolitan Vancouver.   Issues of metropolitan area planning and governance will no doubt become acute as the suburbs demand their due.

It is telling that only recently was there a name change of the whole urban area - from the "Greater Vancouver Regional District" to

"Metro Vancouver". Moving from a "Regional District" to a "Metropolis" is the first step in accepting the new reality. The question, however, is how long will it take for those privileged to govern Vancouver proper, and those privileged to live there, to really accept that there is now one "metropolis", one large important city, where all residents should be concerned about all other residents, and no one group can pretend any longer that, in essence, it is possible to love just the face and not the body.

Metro Vancouver, and its predecessor, the Greater Vancouver Regional District, have been attempting to undertake some planning on a regional scale without sufficient regulatory powers. It is clear that proper planning for Greater Vancouver will require regional government reform as to both planning policy and governance. In the past, regional plans called for a variety of urban centres linked by public transit and roads. However, as Bob Ransford has pointed out, in a column in *The Vancouver Sun* on November 24, 2007, "the planning and management of transit and transportation have been vested over time with either the provincial government or with both the province and a second regional authority disconnected from the metropolitan region's government. Some rapid transit infrastructure exists in the region, but not enough ... (C)ommon sense says transportation planning and land-use planning need to be linked. The same body should be responsible for both – a new Metro Vancouver body."

Ransford makes a good recommendation, if the local politicians can be persuaded that the best interests of their residents depend on regional co-ordination of policies commensurate with the regional nature of the problems: He argues that provincial growth management legislation needs to require each community to accept its share of growth without sprawl, by allocating growth in projected population to the various municipalities, who would be responsible to create the requisite zoned land. The municipalities would still control local planning and zoning within the municipality, but by yielding control of planning for public transit and growth management to the regional level, the planning process can deal more effectively with the true nature of Vancouver as a regional centre. While there has recently been some reform of

TransLink, the Greater Vancouver Transportation Authority, it remains to be seen whether the City of Vancouver as the "face" can integrate itself with the suburban "body", and accept the shift of power that would entail. Unfortunately, there is something of a history of the Provincial Government just stepping into regional matters, when it perceives that the cities are not progressing in the desired way. On November 29, 2007 the BC Government abolished the board of elected municipal politicians that used to make regional transportation decisions at TransLink. It replaced this board with an appointed private sector board, not accountable in itself to the public through a democratic process, but more accountable to provincial policy-making.

Then, in January, 2008, the provincial government unveiled an ambitious and progressive public transit plan, which it projects will cost some $14 billion dollars if all aspects of the plan are built over the next 12 years. It proposed finishing the eastward 11-kilometre Evergreen Line between Lougheed Town Centre and Coquitlam Centre by 2014, a 12-kilometre western extension from Vancouver Community College to the University of British Columbia by 2020, and a 6-kilometer southeasterly extension of the Expo Line to Guildford in Surrey by 2020. In addition, it plans for a "rapid bus system" which would run on dedicated lanes, with signal priority for intersections, and boarding of passengers from raised platforms.

The major initial problem with this otherwise good plan is that the provincial government is only committing itself to 40 percent of the funding, relying on its hope that TransLink, the federal government and the municipalities will supply the balance. Of the $14 billion (at present) price tag, the provincial Premier expects $2.75 billion to come from TransLink, the financially strapped transit entity, and a further $500 million from muncipalities, which of course will be reluctant to raise property taxes, especially the City of Vancouver. Of course it is the funding question that will decide how far this public transit system will go to restoring social justice for working people who need to get around without the adverse financial and environmental and congestion effects of using the private automobile.

If this new public transit is inadequately funded by governments, then it is inevitable that the "Vancouver Model" of dense, yet unaffordable, primarily one and two bedroom condos, will simply spread along the transit stops.   This is because there will be pressure from the City of Vancouver, and perhaps other municipalities, to make up the cost shortfalls by creating partnerships with private developers and sale of increased density.

We shall see in later chapters that Vancouverism supports density as long as someone else pays for the amenities and infrastructure, so that the costs are not passed on to the existing homeowners by way of increased property taxes, but are passed on to the new residents by obligating the developers to pay for amenities like parks and even libraries.   If the developers are going to pay for part of the cost of the transit, then the new condos, especially those close to transit stations, will be priced no more affordably than the new Downtown Vancouver high rise condos, which are now being sold at $800 per square foot, clearly outside the range of affordability.   The developers will pass the costs to the purchasers.

To put it simply, the future of Greater Vancouver as a place that is financially friendly to young working families, who will be able to afford homes in more affordable areas of Greater Vancouver, is threatened by the potential reliance on the private sector developers to fund the transit lines that will make the increased density marketable.

There will be no incentive for municipalities to give incentives to keep the new dense housing along the transit line affordable, and there will be every reason to sell off what will become expensive sites to the same big developers who have brought us Downtown Vancouver.

It is inevitable, in my view, that the very system of growth in housing and public transportation contains within it the source of high housing prices.   The cost of growth of the housing sector and the public transit sector should be shared by all, not just the medium income people who are forced by Vancouver's high prices to move to the suburbs.   The established residents of Vancouver are more than happy with the wild inflation of their housing prices, as if they did the work to justify them.

I argue that in return for the huge tax-free capital gains that these residents will be obtaining, that they share the burden of funding housing and transit, which after all, might be needed by their own children, as well as other people's children and new immigrants.

I would argue as well that failure by any local municipality to create affordable housing by local programs should result in provincial or regional imposed programs.

Unfortunately, narcissistic Vancouverites are insufficiently caring about these others, and therefore do not wish to fund in any way the construction of affordable housing, if there is a cost to them.

The issues are becoming more acute all the time. The narcissistic Vancouverites celebrate their childless downtown and are content with the fact that family-friendly housing in the City is so expensive it forces young families out to the suburbs. Then they look down their noses at the suburbanites for their use of fossil fuels to get their cars into the City. Now, there are concerns that we have attained "peak oil" – i.e. that we are into a world of declining oil resources. Accordingly, these suburbanites face a future of ever-increasing costs of transportation along with the ever-increasing disdain of their City-neighbours for the choice (that they had to make, if they were going to create families) of moving to the suburbs.

To understand the depth of the disdain that Vancouverites now feel towards their suburban neighbours, just read a report by Vancouver architect Richard Balfour, presented to Metro Vancouver, called *Metro Hill Towns For Sustainable Futures.* This report speculates that with ever increasing fuel prices, not only will suburban living become untenable (and the prices of the housing fall, as a consequence), but due to the rising costs of transporting imported food as well due to fuel price hikes, we shall need to, in essence "take back" the suburban land and put it back into agriculture.

The suburban populations, argues Balfour, might have to be clustered in compact settlements in the hills, looking down on the former suburbs, now transformed back into farmland. Is Balfour worried about the fate of these suburbanites? He writes:

"Many people who can afford nothing better or are not yet offered livable sustainable options are going to be hit hard by the changes coming. Who wants to admit that the suburban dream home cannot be heated, you cannot afford to commute to work, the schools are too far away and so are the stores, that nobody wants to buy your house?"

And then the real kicker, showing the elitist Vancouverite view of the suburbanites:

"We can only hope that the pressures that affect change, cause abandonment of suburbs, high rises and strip malls *allow for graceful adaption.* (my emphasis)"

So, Vancouverites, having creating negligible affordable housing for the last twenty years, and thus forcing young families into the suburban municipalities, which have a dearth of rapid transit because Vancouverites don't really want to contribute any tax money to such transit, will now shed nary a tear as the suburbanite dream implodes due to the problem of peak oil.   A narcissistic view of Vancouver means that we mistakenly believe Vancouver stops at our municipal boundaries.   Great cities, truly great cities, places that call themselves the "best place on earth" should stop pretending that suburb and city, Surrey and Vancouver, are separate places, and start working together for the benefit of all.

Anyone truly concerned about the fate of young working people and new immigrants would have to be alarmed at the virtual *assault* on these groups by the lack of an affordable housing policy for low to mid-income working people.   This has worked in tandem with Provincial government policies to weaken the Employment Standards Act by reducing the number of workers covered by the legislation, and the protections to those who remain covered, and by reducing the budget for enforcement of the legislation.

The lack of concern with where our children will live is mirrored by changes to the Employment Standards Act that allow children as young as 12 to be employed for up to 4 hours on a school day, up to 20 hours per week. Is this a tacit admission that 12 year olds are being called on to meet the rent or mortgage money?

Immigrant women are now working for as low as $6. per hour, as a result of the Province allowing this low hourly wage for a "first job" extending up to the first 500 hours of work. How many are really graduating up to more than $6. afterwards?

The effect of this, together with a moving away from unionized manufacturing jobs to "service" jobs and agricultural jobs, has been that in British Columbia the median *real* wage dropped 11.3% from 1980 to the time of the 2006 census on income. ("Labour policies have dramatic influence on wage gap", Professor Marjorie Griffin Cohen, *The Vancouver Sun*, May 22, 2008.) And so the gap between the rich property owners and everyone else widens.

The fate of Vancouver does have national significance for Canada. Our cultural elites have manifested for years a mild (and sometimes not so mild) anti-Americanism as a central component of our national identity. Vancouver stands not so much for the proposition that Canada has produced a "global" or "world-class" city. (The city is far too young for that.) Instead to the horror of the "Starbucks' Progressives, about whom we shall read in Chapter 11, Vancouver is turning into a prosperous American city, like Boston or San Francisco, more than an international city. Absent traditional Canadian virtues like fairness and modesty, the narcissistic New City of Vancouver, has adopted the worst excesses, and the worst social and economic inequities, of any American city. And putting the rich Downtown, rather than the suburbs, will not change that.

Consider the mindset that put the slogan in B.C. government material and on the B.C. special Olympic license plates, "The Best Place on Earth". Sadly, it is all about *recognition, branding,* and *boasting.*

Sadly, this is based on the ideology of the Lotos, and we shall explore this more in future chapters.   Once the Lotos Eaters got a good place on the beach, they did not much care where anyone else lived.   And how easy was it for Vancouver's Lotos Eaters to go from calling their place of residence, "Beautiful B.C." to calling it "The Best Place on Earth".

Excessive narcissism was bad for Ellison.   Eventually, it will be bad for Vancouver.

The boasting about being the best place on earth is so sad.   As Aeschines, the first century (B.C.) Greek statesman and orator said,

"Men of real merit, and whose noble and glorious deeds we are ready to acknowledge, are yet not to be endured when they vaunt their own actions."

And these are the famous words of William Shakespeare from *All's Well That Ends Well:*

"It will come to pass that every braggart shall be found an ass."

Chapter 4

Lusting for Location: The Sexualization of Shelter

"What do college students talk about with their roommates? Sex. Twenty years later, what do they talk about with their friends and associates? Real estate. And with the same gleam in the eyes. Real estate today has become a form of yuppie pornography".

-Marjorie Garber, *Sex and Real Estate: Why We Love Houses*

Real Estate has always been the primary way to denote status. A portfolio of blue-chip stocks is one thing, but the "dream home" is much more visible. Today's male wants a big house (or big condo) the way yesterday's male wanted a big automobile or a big cigar; symbol of power and wealth, or simply phallic symbol, it is all the same. Today's female also seeks confirmation of her status, whether as high income earner herself, or as having had the goods to attract the man who could provide such accommodation.

Yet as Professor Garber duly notes, in the quote above, real estate has moved into almost a sexual realm, in her words, "yuppie pornography". This is the age of the internet, where every kind of nude photo or image of any sexual conduct imaginable, is available by hitting a few buttons. One wonders, at some point, do the varieties of the nude body, and its erotic capabilities tend to bore the internet voyeur, to be replaced by the kind of "virtual tours" of other people's homes, now available from many real estate brokerage sites. Has our accommodation passed from shelter to erotic image and in turn to romantic and sexual fulfillment?

Professor Garber's book is quite an achievement. Look at how she starts Chapter One, entitled, "The House As Beloved - *Falling In Love With A House*:

"Anyone who doubts the possibility of falling in love with a house - with all that implies of fast-beating heart, sweaty palms, and waiting for the phone to ring - just hasn't met the right one yet."

Has our preference for convenient access to amenities and our preference for a pretty view transcended mere *preference* – are we now *lusting* for *location*?

As Vancouver real estate agent Luigi Frascati, who writes a weblog about real estate, has said: "There is so much money around, and buyers want to flaunt it. They will swear and they will protest and say they do not want to show off, but they do. They want a house that makes a clear, undeniable statement that 'I am rich', 'I have prosperity' and 'I have style'."

Mr. Frascati, however, is more than a casual observer of his client's desire to show off. He writes evocatively of how design elements reflect masculine and feminine aspects:

"Architectural styles of new constructions are changing and evolving, with the ever increasing round looks of exteriors that reflect feminine sensuality and the use of glazed windows and conspicuous steel beams - male machismo at its best. On the inside, the skillful blend of colors, woods and design elements promotes feminine harmony, warmth and balance with char green, sand, white, red, black, dark brown and all colors of nature at the top of the line whereas, if contemplating a hardwood floor, mahogany is the wood of choice since it enriches the environment by rendering a sense of abundance, and slate flooring and polished concrete walls help create a natural masculine feeling, especially if combined and contrasted with the glacial looks of stainless steel appliances."

Of course, such a categorization of masculine versus feminine is quite incorrect in Vancouver, in that the sizable gay/lesbian/transgendered community can rightly correct a too-narrow view of masculinity and femininity. Moreover, sexualization of shelter is the great equalizer between gays and straights – we may not agree on which gender we covet, but we can agree on what homes turn us on.

Vancouver, with its beautiful mountain and water views is particularly susceptible to a type of lust to have an unblocked, 24 hour a day, view that will "take your breath away" or provide such other reactions formerly limited to the romantic and erotic effects of love.

Let's look at how some of Vancouver's new (predominantly condo) real estate developments are being marketed (names of buildings and developers omitted):

A new Downtown building with luxury hotel rooms on the first 26 floors and condos priced from $2.25 million to $10 million on floors 27 to 60: "The world's finest hotel company...The World's finest city".

A Burnaby tower: "... is designed to bring all that matters to you right to your fingertips ... (the) kitchen is ready to sizzle no matter how demanding the chef may be."

Describing a 146 unit development, adjacent to Simon Fraser University as a "sizzling" new addition to the area, the marketers headline their ad: "Vivacious, gregarious, and eclectic."

A downtown Vancouver project in upscale Coal Harbour, with condos starting at $1.5 million dollars, promises buyers that they can "Live the View", whatever that means.

A new building in False Creek, on the waterfront, promises buyers "A World Address", (not just a Vancouver address, however that works).

Several ads for buildings in different neighbourhoods all promise the buyers that they will be living in Vancouver's "hottest neighbourhood".

A new condo development near Chinatown (and thus also near the Downtown East Side) calls its homes "zesty" and promises a location "loaded with worldly pleasures".

A Kitsilano high rise promises "a home distinct as you are."

And in the October 12, 2007 issue of NewHome Buyer's Guide, (which covers not only Vancouver but all the surrounding suburban towns in the Fraser Valley, Burnaby, North Shore, down to Surrey and out to Abbotsford (125 pages of advertisements, photos and advertorials), I counted only 7 photos that included children of any age in them. There were no children in any of the photos for the Vancouver buildings, all seven photos were for family housing in the outlying area. Obviously, children detract from the sexy promise of the idealized and sexualized living space.

So, why does this matter, anyway? Why should we worry if people are investing so much of themselves into their homes? Why should it be our concern if the home is as much a sexual object as a person?

The problem is that sexual attraction is not very logical. The Divorce Courts know all about the problems that arise if the initial sexual attraction starts to diminish and the couple realize that they really don't like each other as people. If our culture conduces to decisions on shelter based on the sexiness of the view, the erotic master bedroom ensuite "retreat", or the coveted street address, our homebuyers are going to forget about a lot of other things, in their rush of passion.

You see, Real Estate is a fickle lover. Notwithstanding the hype promoted by real estate agents and the advertorials in the subservient media (gorging itself on real estate advertising revenue), real estate prices go up and also *go down.* When the American dollar goes down, and the U.S. house market goes down, and when the U.S. moves into a recession, fewer Americans will buy Vancouver area properties and more will try to cash in on the increased value of their investments relative to the U.S. dollar. There is such a thing as a recession. In an increasingly unstable world, with "peak oil" in the hands of unstable regimes, we are subject to economic forces beyond our control. A recession in the U.S. and a steep decline in real estate wealth there, will in fact have some effects in British Columbia. We shall soon start to see new condo projects being cancelled or running into financial problems. Some of the purchasers will forfeit their deposits, and try to "disappear", leaving the developer with useless contracts. Some of the fanciest condos marketed to Asians who have lost millions in the decline of the Chinese stock market, or Russian oligarchs who are being wiped out financially, will also face problems.

Real estate values are in large measure driven by psychology. When people are confident about their jobs, their income and political and economic stability, they can buy into the relatively absurd notion that real estate values have nowhere to go but up. They forget about the previous bubbles that have burst. And the real estate agents feed the euphoria of rising markets. I was astounded at what I saw here in 2006 to early 2008, when agents were telling buyers not to put any conditions in their offers, because the sellers would not accept conditional offers. In other words, in a city where numerous buyers had been devastated by poor construction practices (like the leaky condos which we shall discuss more later), real estate agents created a system where purchasers were blindly buying the largest purchase of their lives, without protective conditions for a house inspection to look for defects in construction. Real estate agents were participating in a corrupted system where young buyers were advised that the market was so hot that houses would be going for a hundred thousand dollars or more over listing price. One week after listing, the seller would review the dozen or so unconditional offers collected, and then the lucky buyer with the most astute agent (who had advised to go over the listing price by the most absurd sum) would get a house and the privilege to see how many tens (or hundreds) of thousands of dollars of renovations might be necessary on top of the already obscene price.

Then when the psychology changes, for example, when oil prices rise dramatically, or when people open their eyes to the political and economic dangers lurking around the corner, prices start to nosedive rather quickly. The same real estate agents who promoted the earlier hype, and profited so handsomely with large commissions, now turn to pressuring sellers to sell at a "realistic" price to get rid of their properties before prices go even lower.

Essentially, we allow real estate agents to play games with hundreds of thousands of dollars of people's money that we would never tolerate with used car salesmen selling $5,000 used cars.

When real estate development and construction begin to dominate the economy, a recession can get very deep very fast, because so many people rely on the sector for jobs and income – not just construction workers, but all the material suppliers and sub-trades, realtors, consulting planners, lawyers, bankers etc. Then there are the people who sell pickup trucks to the builders, and the other suppliers of the suppliers. One can look at South Florida as an example of a place that has little industry, but is based on services and real estate construction for the vast number of people who retire there. However, once real estate slows down, the repercussions in such an economy are vast – the "bubble" bursts. Vancouver is more susceptible to "bubbling" than many people think.

As of the time of writing this (June, 2008) the first signs of a slowdown are appearing: The B.C. Real Estate Association reported that May, 2008 sales were off 31 percent compared to May, 2007, and listings rose 38% between May, 2007 and May, 200

Moreover, poor construction techniques for the prevention of water leakage into units has been a virtual epidemic. The "leaky condo" fiasco in Vancouver was so extensive, and continues to haunt so many condo owners who cannot afford the necessary repairs, that you would think that people would be reluctant to buy *any* condos in Vancouver. But when the mainstream press relies on advertising dollars from the same developers who have so fundamentally failed their customers for years, then the leaky condo story tends not to be covered anymore, although new problems continue to arise in existing buildings. It has all been papered over by media and real estate agent hype, blinding customers to the inherent fundamental faults of their Real Estate loves.

And when you are in *love* the world looks different.

For example, in Downtown Vancouver, new condos range from $750 per square foot and up. That means a small one bedroom will be over $300,000 and a modest two bedroom will be over $500,000. As discussed earlier, the size of the units do not make it possible to have much in the way of a family. And as noted above, the advertising doesn't purport to hold these units out to be family housing; children are just left out of the picture. As we shall discuss in Chapter 9, this is part and parcel of the ideology of the Lotos.

In times past, some housing was fairly flexible. Parts of the house could be rented out until the family grew into the whole house, and then later as children grew up, part of the house could be portioned off for the child's family, or part could be rented out again. The high priced condo units, with their high-end granite, hardwood flooring and luxury plumbing fixtures, are not meant to be flexible.

Even worse, they are sold on the basis of high end finishings. In years' past a young couple might forgo anything but the most basic kitchen and bath, just to get into a home, that they could afford, and then upgrade things as future income would permit. Now, however, the buyer is lured into a highly finished expensive unit, and, when it is no longer suitable, the "move up" involves an addition of hundreds of thousands of dollars to the mortgage and payment of real estate commission on the unit sold. It hardly seems an efficient way to provide for housing.

Architectural writer Lance Berelowitz, interviewed by David Beers in *The Tyee*, May 25, 2005, makes the point: "We've put a significant concentration of this form (one and two bedroom condo towers) in large areas all at once. By all at once, I mean the last 20 – 25 years, which in the scheme of city-making is a blink of an eye. Great swaths of the city have been recreated with this new product. And now people talk about that as the 'Vancouver Model'."

Continues Berelowitz: "I am more interested in how we use the city than necessarily how it looks. The American architect Andres Duany, one of the godfathers of new urbanism, was in Vancouver briefly, and he made the point that these towers are incredibly inflexible. He noted that unlike the brownstone apartment buildings of Boston, New York or Montreal, or the row housing of Victorian London or the inner-ring suburbs of a place like Toronto, Vancouver's towers were custom designed for one thing and one thing only, and when and if we want to change them in 10 or 20 or 30 or 50 years time, there is going to be hell to pay."

Instead of a variety of housing, capable of being organic and changeable over time, Vancouver has created a sanitized, uni-dimensional Downtown, supposedly in a sustainable and environmentally way, to meet the needs of the increasing population drawn to "the best place on earth".   The problem, however, is that Vancouver has chosen a "sexy" product over a utilitarian one. $300,000 one bedrooms and $700,000 two bedrooms hardly seem to serve the entire spectrum of housing needs, especially those who have, or intend to have, children, and those who are looking for a $300,000 *three bedroom.*

Moreover, there is something very interesting happening in that area of Downtown Vancouver, south of Robson, East of Burrard, extending eastward to Pacific Blvd. and almost to B.C. Place.   This 35 hectare area, now called "Downtown South" is not a master-planned community like the Concord Pacific buildings on the former Expo '86 lands.   Nor does it have the cachet of Yaletown or Gastown.   As Frances Bula pointed out in an article in *The Vancouver Sun* in January, 2008, individual condo developers have erected within the 34 blocks of Downtown South some 46 high-rise towers, with 15 more under construction, and plans to turn the remaining parking lots and one-storey buildings into more.

What is interesting to me is how the city planners, so swept away by the vision of the Vancouver Model, erred so substantially in their plans. The planners were planning for a total eventual population of 14,000, but now admit that the population should reach 24,000 by 2021, making it twice as dense as the West End of downtown, long considered the most dense area in Canada.

What this means to the residents is that the city is now scrambling to provide the appropriate level of services to such a large mass of people. There are inadequate parks and schools. Yes, schools. While little has been done to make Downtown South truly child-friendly, there is still demand from young families to live there. However, a community of some 15,000 people (at present) only has one existing school to serve it. Elsie Roy School is overburdened, and parents must camp out overnight before registration day to get their children the few precious spots in the kindergarten program. Even though there are so few affordable condo apartments sized for families and even though the landscape contains little grass or trees, and is dominated by major thoroughfares, the demand by families to live somewhere Downtown, and the provision of a few hundred social housing units in the new developments, have now resulted in some 600 children residing there.

One really has to wonder about a planning process that was so uncaring about children. Of course, since Tennyson's Lotos Eaters decided to *abandon* their children, we should not be so surprised. Yet, in the real world of Vancouver, there are certain realities that are not being addressed:

No doubt doing without the expense of keeping a car on the road, enough young couples want to bring their growing families downtown to escape the commute. Yes, the Vancouver Model has created more residential than anything else. However, there are still a lot of people who work downtown, and it seems like a reasonable thing for young families, where both parents work downtown, to live downtown. But for now, the planners seem to be surprised that there are indeed young families who can afford the new condos. In the article by Frances Bula, she refers to "an almost desperate-sounding report to council" by central-area planner David Ramslie, stating that while the city had promised to provide 2.8 hectares of park space in the area, it had so far only provided .53 hectares. Bula notes also that while the city had planned to create 189 child-care spaces by 2007, in fact only 74 had been created. Ramslie's report concluded it would take some $80 million to provide the missing parks, child care, social housing, and street improvements that the area needed by 2021. The problem is that Council dares not ask the general tax base to pay increased property taxes so that the denizens of Downtown South can have a decent lifestyle. Instead, as usual, development cost charges were substantially increased, thus making the new apartments even less affordable than they would otherwise be. The residents of Lotus Land get a warm feeling when they see new Downtown condos going for high prices because it raises the values of their single family homes or condos.

The social justice problem is that the existing residents have no problem accepting the increased property values of their own houses that result from the new buildings' increased selling prices, but cry in protest if they are asked to bear any portion of these costs.

Surely, most new buyers of housing in Vancouver do not understand that the obscene prices charged for new condos are in part caused by the unwillingness of existing residents to make financial contributions through property taxes towards the cost of parks and other facilities for them, leaving the future residents to be passed such costs as part of the purchase price. And they do not understand that this inappropriate form of real estate, with neighbourhoods which are unfriendly to young families, was never really designed for them anyway. They were designed, in the mythology of the Vancouver Model, for the global crowd that supposedly makes Vancouver the World City that it claims to be. Instead, they fall prey to a sophisticated marketing blitz to convince them, with sexy advertisements and beautifully designed model suites, that they are getting their money's worth when they fork over $700 to $800 per square foot.

It is a crazy world where the interior designer of the model suite is touted as much as the name of the builder. The art of making the show suite so attractive is surely a transparent attempt at deflecting the attention of the buyer from the fact that the small one and two bedrooms no longer have a separate kitchen – the kitchen is simply at the end of the living room. The disadvantage of an open kitchen exposing your dirty dishes off to your dinner guests is seen to be overcome by the advantage of the "open concept". The interior designer creates the fantasy being marketed.

Of course, unless our politicians and urban planners step up to the plate and do their job, there is no morality in real estate; there are no *values* except the worship of "property *values*". Arguably, by ignoring our own future residents' needs, in favour of the needs of developers, investors, wealthy older owners of existing properties, speculators and the international market, we have ill-served the moral needs of *our entire* society.

The data is not all readily available. But we do know, from a study by Landcor Data Corp. (quoted in *The Vancouver Sun* on November 19, 2007) that in B.C., as a whole, in October 2007, there are 13,972 properties registered to American domiciled owners. Add to that the number of properties owned by Chinese and other Asian investors. If we simply allow the "market" to determine what we create in terms of housing, we are not only ignoring our own working classes, but we are aiming to serve people who are not even *Canadians.*

We have, as a society, abnegated our planning process in favour of the supposed demands of the "market." Instead of planning for affordable housing, with any of the dozens of affordable housing inducement programs being used to great success in Ontario or the United States, we have bought into the sexy vision of Vancouver as a "global" centre, where thousands and thousands of international entrepreneurs are attracted to keeping condo apartments in our sexy Downtown by the Sea.

However, many units in each new development are bought by speculators who then re-sell or "assign" their purchase contracts, and many are bought by investors, who, in the few years before they plan to sell for a capital gain, rent out their units. These rental units are of course "unsustainable" because they are to be sold in a few years, and are an inefficient response to the need for dedicated and affordable rental housing.

Moreover, there is the issue of "unoccupied" condos. Anyone who lives downtown will attest to the fact that close to 25% of the downtown condos don't even appear to be occupied. Are these held by speculators? Are they owned by people who use them only a few weeks a year?   Or perhaps some are purchased by organized crime and drug-lords as part of the money-laundering of proceeds of crime and drug deals?

Gregor Robertson, shortly after being selected as the Vision Vancouver candidate for mayor, did a radio interview where he mentioned that some 18,000 downtown condos had been sold to investors who were keeping them empty, satisfied to make a substantial capital gain, if the prices keep rising.   Robertson advocates a wonderful policy evidencing the single most progressive thinking that Vancouver has seen in the last few years: He suggests that since these units are a business investment and no one lives there, they should not get the benefit of low residential property taxes but should be taxed as business properties.   Bravo!

Everyone knows that land in Vancouver is a scarce and diminishing resource.   Everyone knows that the main reason for the huge inflation of housing prices is the inflation of the land value.   Most simple bungalows in Vancouver anywhere west of Main Street are worth the same as their land value; that is, just over $1 million dollars with or without the bungalow.

While Vancouver City Council, and its Planning Department, were bowled over by the sexy high rise condo units and the "Vancouver Model", someone forgot to set aside a sufficient portion of land to take "off market" for one of the several forms of off-market housing being created with such success elsewhere.   In particular, I would cite the example of the hundreds of Community Housing Trusts (sometimes called Community Land Trusts) recently created in the U.S., and even in some places in Canada (for example, Canmore Alberta - where a wonderful project is owned by the municipal housing corporation, rather than a separate Trust, and carries the title of "Perpetually Affordable Housing").

The land for these Housing Trusts in bought by muncipalities, sponsoring non-profit organizations, unions, or other interested parties. Municipalities can establish Affordable Housing Funds, which take contributions from regular housing developers on a per unit basis, or by depositing "demolition taxes" each time an affordable older home is demolished to make way for expensive new housing,   These Affordable Housing Funds, whatever the source of their funding, can be used to buy and hold title to public Community Housing Trusts. But whether the title is held by the municipality or by some other organization, the method is to have a variety of housing built, with long term leases, and restrictive covenants limiting the selling price of the units, to some pre-determined formula, which might take into effect inflation or buyer improvements, but not the future inflation of land values.   Essentially the land values become fixed in time, thus preserving future affordability of the units in the Housing Trust, even in a City that has run out of land.

The owner of a unit in the Community Housing Trust will normally be eligible if his or her family income is a certain percentage of the average mean income (AMI) in the municipality, often fixed in the neighbourhood of 80% to 100% of AMI in the case of rented units, or from 100% right up to 200% of AMI in the case of owned units.

Vancouver, which has the highest real estate values in the country, does not have the highest AMI in the country; far from it – Vancouver's AMI is approximately $55,000.   And given current property values, which require an income of about $130,000 to service a mortgage on a modest Vancouver east-end bungalow, there is thus the need to help those whose income is twice the AMI.

Unfortunately, Vancouver and British Columbia, for all the boasting about the Vancouver Model, lag just about everywhere in North America in terms of affordable housing programs, especially those that induce the private sector to act to create new affordable rental units. The Community Housing Trust is one model that I think holds great promise for an inherently inflationary market like Vancouver, where the quality of life, the climate, and the scenery will all cause a continuing immigration to the area.

Instead of such supply-oriented programs, we have instead artificially propped up high prices by the provision of somewhat dangerous supports for increased demand.   The mortgage programs that allow for "no money down", or stretch out the amortization periods from 25 years to 40 years do not really help affordability.   Instead they help maintain high prices as young buyers are induced into financial products that will keep them prisoners of mortgage debt for 40 years, and prevent the rapid pay down of the indebtedness.   Any decline in the market, or any increase in mortgage rates, will produce many casualties among young people whose decision making was skewed by the belief that they should get into the market on any terms before prices go even higher. (Fortunately, Canada Mortgage and Housing Corporation has just cancelled the 40 year amortization program.)

Just as the solution for high rents is inducement programs for the construction of more rental units, the solution for high purchase prices is to let the demand fall and the prices come down.   The provision of off-market housing, such as Community Housing Trusts, is of course part of the solution. However, the wrong approach is to induce young buyers to get in over their heads by "innovative" mortgage products. It is sad to see 40 year olds whose whole purpose in life seems to have been to acquire a Kitsilano half-duplex at $1.2 million with a $600,000 mortgage, while they have foregone having children or pursuing any other of life's major pursuits.

What is needed is some growing up.   We must get away from the notion that real estate is sex;   we must stop sexualizing our shelter. Housing is a basic component of a dignified life.   Let the ultra rich impress each other with the sexiness of their houses;   for the rest of us, we need a change in attitude, leading to a change in product.

We shall return to the issue of housing affordability in Chapter 9.

Chapter 5

Aspects of the Lotos Among the Young and the Old

"Why are we weigh'd upon with heaviness,
And utterly consumed with sharp distress,
While all things else have rest from weariness?
All things have rest: why should we toil alone,
We only toil, who are the first of things,
And make perpetual moan,
Still from one sorrow to another thrown:
Nor ever fold our wings,
And cease from wanderings,
Nor steep our brows in slumber's holy balm;
Nor hearken what the inner spirit sings,
'There is no joy but calm!'
Why should we only toil, the roof and crown of
　　　　things?"

Alfred Tennyson, "The Lotos-Eaters"

Having discussed the basic ideology of the Lotos Eaters, the political culture and priorities of Vancouver as New City, the cultural narcissism, and the cultural importance of upscale housing in Vancouver, we return to a consideration of Tennyson's poem, "The Lotos-Eaters", to see what it can teach us about the cultural "foundation" of *Vancouverism* in the Canadian Lotus Land.

In the poem, the mariners of Odysseus see a land "in which it seemed always afternoon" because of the calm and peaceful atmosphere. Coincidentally, this land has a gleaming *river* flowing to the sea, three snow-capped *mountaintops*, and shadowy *pine* growing in the vale. (Interestingly, Vancouver has a great river flowing to the sea – the Fraser River, and three snow-capped mountains – Grouse Mountain, Cypress Mountain, and Mount Seymour, and the lodgepole pine is the most widespread tree in the province!)

"Mild-eyed melancholy lotos-eaters" bring the flower and fruit of the lotos. The mariners who eat it feel as if they have fallen into a deep sleep, hardly hearing their fellow mariners speaking to them, hearing only the music of their own "beating heart(s)".

Although they dream of returning to their families in Ithaca, the lotos makes them tired of their wandering, and they all say, "we will no longer roam."

The next verse has the mariners praising the beautiful music of the land of the Lotos-Eaters, and comparing it to the beautiful flowers there. And then comes the very remarkable verse quoted at the beginning of this chapter. Why is it so remarkable?

After their ingestion of the lotos, they now question why man is the only creature in nature who must toil. They state that everything else in nature is able to rest, but man is tossed from one sorrow to another. They argue that mankind's "inner spirit sings, 'There is no joy but calm'"; in other words, that tranquility and calmness offer the only joy.

So, here in the land of the Lotos-Eaters, after imbibing the lotos, the great mariners of Ulysses negate any of the great values of life, stating that the only joy comes from calmness. No more labour. Life to be "sweet" will consist of

"hearing the downward stream,
With half-shut eyes ever to seem,
Falling asleep in a half-dream!"

"(And t)o hear each other's whispered speech;
Eating the Lotos day by day,
(and watching) the crisping ripples on the beach."

And then concluding the poem, the mariners state:

"We have had enough of action, and of motion we ...
Let us swear an oath, and keep it with an equal mind,

In the hollow Lotos-land to live and lie reclined
On the hills like gods together, careless of mankind...."

So, enough of "action", enough of "toil"; there is no joy, but in "calm". The mariners plead, "Let us alone"; three times, they state "Let us alone", and then argue that they cannot have pleasure from a "war with evil". In fact, they point out that:

"All things have rest, and ripen toward the grave
In silence, ripen, fall and cease:
Give us long rest or death, dark death, or dreamful ease."

And, thus, we see the ultimate argument of the mariners: even death is preferable to a life of toil, a life of action, and a life of battling evil. Of course, Tennyson intends us to be somewhat shocked by this position. (Note how he uses the adjective "hollow" to describe Lotos-land.) Tennyson, schooled in the stories of the Bible, was no doubt intending that this poem be linked to the story of Adam and Eve and the forbidden fruit of the Tree of Knowledge of Good and Evil, in Genesis, the first book of the Five Books of Moses.

Let us look deeper in our attempt to fully understand Tennyson's poem, and so to understand the real meaning of the concept of "Lotus Land".

Classic Jewish teaching of the Adam and Eve story in the Torah is that God gave them the commandment not to eat the fruit of the Tree of Knowledge of Good and Evil, in order to give them *free will*, and allow them to earn, rather than receive, a higher spiritual state. This teaching states that had they resisted the temptation to eat the forbidden fruit, they would have attained a state of perfection and immortality. But after failing in their test, they were, in essence, condemned by God to a "life of toil". (In Genesis 3:19, Adam is told that because of their transgression, in future he would eat bread only after the "sweat of (his) face".) Moreover, biblical commentators held that this "life of toil" was for the purpose of rectifying the fallen universe, or as it is sometimes stated, to "repair the world". So, Tennyson's mariners, in repudiating a "life of toil" and refusing to combat "evil", by instead partaking of the fruit of the lotos, are in fact repudiating the Biblical essence of the human mission in history, which is to repair the world.

When the mariners turn to the lotos, and use it to achieve "calm" rather than toil to improve the world, they are in Tennyson's poem repudiating a central purpose of humankind's role on earth, according to a traditional Judeo-Christian ethic.

And so, we return to the issue of *Vancouverism*, and to what extent we are a city of Tennyson's mariners, turning to the lotos, as opposed to a life of toil to improve the world. This chapter has been called "Aspects of the Lotos Among the Young and the Old." That is, in examining these two groups in particular, we have the opportunity to understand the extent to which Tennyson's view of the Lotos in fact underpins much of the culture of *Vancouverism.*

For this purpose, we must distinguish between the "old" Vancouver, a city based on forestry, fishing, the railway, and other vocations of hard labour, and the "new" Vancouver, based on the new economy of finance and the stock market, computer technology, bio-technology, international business, video game design, film-making, real estate speculation, and also the simple depositing of business and investment income earned somewhere else. For there is no doubt that sometime in the last twenty years the old Vancouver turned into the new Vancouver.

And, of course, in examining cultural trends, we must acknowledge that these are only *trends*, and at most *prevailing* thought patterns more apropos to Vancouver than other cities: these are not uniform in all of the population. It is obvious that Vancouver has a tremendous number of people seeking to fulfill, through toil, the perfection of the world, and the improvement of social conditions, health, safety, the environment, and social justice. We have a good number of philanthropists. Our inquiry, then, is limited to an exploration of the unique aspects and trends of *Vancouverism*, to better understand the policy choices that have been made in urban politics and planning, and to better understand why Vancouver has become the "Emperor's New City".

For the young, the Lotos in Vancouver is represented, on the one hand, by the proverbial "sex, drugs, and rock 'n' roll", and on the other hand, by Tennyson's description of watching "the crisping ripples on the beach".   There is also, in common with youth elsewhere, something of a worship of "pagan" body art.

For the old, the Lotos in Vancouver is the way its moderate climate and natural beauty make it (along with Victoria and the cities of the Okanagan Valley) the ideal retirement destination for upper income Canadians.   The large demographic group called Baby Boomers (born between 1946 and 1964) started turning 60 in 2006, and hence there will be a large group of new retirees looking at retirement to British Columbia in the next 15 years.

Some retired Canadians will not think of leaving their home towns, where they spent their working lives, made friends, perhaps still have children and grandchildren there. Some of them would not think of leaving their Churches, Temples, Synagogues or Mosques, where they have established their spiritual identities. Some will want to give back to the communities, where they have made their money, some compensation through charitable work or other participation in the non-profit sector.   For these, a three week vacation in Florida or Arizona will suffice.   But there are others, who follow the call of the Lotos:

"We have had enough of action, and of motion we,
… Let us swear an oath, and keep it with an equal mind,
In the hollow Lotos-land to live and lie reclined
On the hills like Gods together, careless of mankind"

Vancouver has the least participation in organized religion of any city in Canada.   Although the 2001 census showed that 43% of Vancouverites stated that they had "no religion", it is not clear if some of those people have a traditional belief in the Divine, or still have a faith that there is some higher purpose to human existence.   Some people state that they are "spiritual" but avoid "organized" religion. At any rate, it is fair to infer that, with such a large percentage of the population stating on surveys that they have "no" religion, potentially a large number of people here take the same view as Tennyson's mariners about the gods "together careless of mankind":

"For they lie beside their nectar, and the bolts are hurl'd
Far below them in the valleys, and the clouds are
          lightly curl'd
Round their golden houses, girdled with the
          gleaming world:
Where they smile in secret, looking over wasted lands,
Blight and famine, plague and earthquake, roaring
          deeps and fiery sands,
Clanging fights, and flaming towns, and sinking
          ships, and praying hands.
But they smile, they find a music centred in a doleful
          song
Steaming up, a lamentation and an ancient tale of
          wrong,
Like a tale of little meaning tho' the words are
          strong;"

And so we see the ideological divide between those who seek out toil to repair the world, and those who see this life as a "tale of little meaning" ruled over by gods who are "careless of mankind" and in fact "smile in secret" as they send to mankind "blight and famine, plague and earthquake...Clanging fights and flaming towns, and sinking ships".

Thus, retirement to fancy condos, luxury yachts, and private golf clubs will give Lotos-toys to those who have earned them, so that the terrible thoughts of our meaningless existence can be held at bay. I read their minds: "Never mind issues like terrorism and Islamo-fascism...those things are so far away.   If we Canadians live our quiet lives on our sail boats and golf courses, then what do we have to fear?…..It is such an *American* or *European* problem.", they seem to say.

Is it any wonder that the *Vancouver Sun* rarely has any international news or world issues on its front page? The front page is given over, almost exclusively, to local issues. In a world in crisis, with culture wars and daily terrorist massacres, the denizens of Vancouver appear preoccupied with the local, preoccupied with the Lotos.

In this, they are closer than they believe to the young, who have a certain segment who are so obviously addicted to sex, drugs, rock 'n' roll and the beaches. For the young, we may consider that it has been forever thus. But the young in Vancouver face a very uncertain future in terms of secure employment and affordable housing. The Lotos can offer an escape, albeit temporary. We shall return to this issue in Chapter 9.

At the same time, Vancouver has a concentrated district of bars serving mainly the young, politely termed the "Granville Street entertainment district". On a Saturday night after 11:00 p.m. there is nothing better about this "entertainment district" than there is about the Downtown Eastside. Youthful revellers who have spent 3 or 4 hours drinking, will sometimes resort to street brawls. The scene is not pretty. A gentleman named Ned Jacobs (which is the name of Jane Jacobs' son) writing a letter to the editor of *The Vancouver Sun* on November 19th, 2007, correctly framed the problem. He wrote: "The Granville entertainment district is a temple to bad behaviour because principles of sound planning were ignored from the start." He quotes Jane Jacobs from her *Dark Age Ahead:* "In cities, differing uses in close proximity tame one another." Yet in Lotus Land, the creation of a large district mainly devoted to the consumption of alcohol passes for "entertainment". Bad planning, indeed.

And yet, planning in the Lotus land may be a contradiction in terms. The Lotos emphasizes calm, tranquility, inaction, and beauty. In fact, the land is most beautiful without *any* people populating it. The more we populate it, then by definition it becomes less beautiful, less calm and less tranquil. That is the fundamental contradiction in the idea of the Lotos;   how do you plan for that very thing that you really want the least?   How do you reconcile beauty and increased population? Thus, many of the most lotus-like of Vancouverites have withdrawn to low density living on the Gulf Islands.   In Chapter 14, we shall deal with the issue of how does a culture factor in the concept of social justice, when its values are primarily esthetic.

As to the older generations, is it really true that Vancouverism emphasizes the parochial and de-emphasizes the great international issues of our times?   I shall answer this by recounting an experience at a dinner-party I attended, not long after moving to Vancouver.

In a group, above average in education, in income, in both home and boat ownership, I made the mistake of articulating some of my concerns about the effects of terrorism on our political culture.   I decided to mention how surprised I was on a recent ferry crossing to Vancouver Island that the huge ferry boats, taking hundreds of cars and passengers between Vancouver and Victoria, and other sites on Vancouver Island and the Gulf Islands, seemed to have no security against terrorist attack.

I mentioned how susceptible these ferries would be to a very unsophisticated terrorist attack, where some nefarious group could drive a van or car onto the ferry, filled with enough explosives to sink the ferry.

As I stated this, one fellow diner, became more and more agitated, till he blurted out, "I think we have heard enough from you."   He couldn't think of any rebuttal or comment, except that he did not want me to say anything more about a subject that was making him too uncomfortable. This man, a former corporate executive, who had fled corporate life, to become a boat-builder, and was substantially addicted to marijuana, was livid that I could even suggest that his Lotos might be subject to the same threats being taken seriously all over the Western World.

It was my first indication that *Vancouverism* was a very different state of mind.

Chapter 6

Resort Lobbies, Doggie Spas and Affordable Housing

"Perhaps it hasn't one," Alice ventured to remark. "Tut, tut, child!" said the Duchess. "Everything's got a moral, if only you can find it."

- Lewis Carroll, *Alice in Wonderland*

I have just returned to Vancouver from the 7 days per month I spend in Ontario where I develop affordable rental housing for working people of modest incomes. My group usually does a couple of buildings per year. Last year, we converted a 130 year old Church in Brantford Ontario (a city of 100,000 one hour from Toronto) into 17 units with all-inclusive rents of $630 per month for a one-bedroom and $680 per month for a two-bedroom. This year we are converting a heritage two-storey brick warehouse building into 28 units with the same rental structure, and another former Church in Woodstock Ontario. These three projects are done under a program of forgivable loans, made available to private sector companies willing to adhere to 15 year agreements specifying allowable rents and income levels for the tenants. We have also done projects under a wonderful program called the Canada-Ontario Affordable Housing Partnership, which is designed to give forgivable loans to those building new affordable rental buildings. These projects are done under programs that do not exist in British Columbia.

My wife often cuts out some articles from the *Sun* that have run during my absence, which she figures I might find interesting.

First, from the January 15, 2007, edition, a story about how house prices on the North Shore are well out of reach for police officers who work in West Vancouver. Accordingly, West Vancouver is having trouble attracting, and retaining, police officers who usually make under $100,000, and therefore can't live there. Assuming that this is a problem in many areas of Vancouver, and assuming that police officers are at the upper income level for many in our "workforce", this reflects a new reality - Vancouver has created a housing market which is too rich for the workforce that makes our daily life possible. All those who may have, in the last few months, ever uttered such words as 'sustainability" or "social justice" might want to reflect on the nature of a society that doesn't care about housing its workforce anywhere near where they work.

Second, from the January 18th edition, a feature story about upscale dog hotels, spas, photographic studios and grooming salons. It appears that there is a significant market for those who want to spend $150 to have Fido's hair, ears, nails, etc. done up with style. Then the dog can be professionally photographed for $300, and when its owners are out of town, it can stay at a "dog hotel" with rates *starting* at $60 per night.

I suppose the only downside about being a dog in Vancouver is having to share the sidewalks with homeless people sleeping under pieces of plastic.

Third, the *piece de resistance* – an article in the *Westcoast Homes* section by Vancouver "architect, planner and property developer" Michael Geller, entitled "Designers can learn from resort lobbies". Mr. Geller, now traveling around the world, is going to be, according to the article's introduction, sharing his "discoveries" with readers. And what is the very first discovery in which Vancouverites are privileged to share? Well, according to Mr. Geller, it appears that what we need to know is that the design of a lobby of a luxury resort in Fiji can teach us important lessons on residential design.

First, a little context. I looked up on the internet, the room rates for the resort in question, the Fiji Sheraton: the best deal I could find is about $300 per night in Fiji dollars, which is over $200 per night in Canadian dollars.

A little lesson I have learned from developing affordable housing – there is no budget, zero budget, *nada*, for a lobby. I find that room for a mailbox is greatly appreciated, and if our units feature separate bedrooms rather than Murphy beds, the tenants are thrilled.

But Mr. Geller laments the lack of attention to parking garage "lobbies": he boasts how he has used crown moldings and wall coverings for his parking lobbies. No wonder, then, that workforce housing is not being produced in Vancouver: our best minds are apparently figuring out how to further "upscale" front lobbies to match those of luxury resorts, and how to make parking lobbies win urban design awards.

But what can we really expect in a province that has just upped the housing price limit for obtaining a property tax rebate, from $950,000 to $1,050,000? And what can we expect from a city whose idea of promoting affordability is promoting "density" - through high rise condos with mainly one bedroom apartments, and little in the way of true "family" housing, (that would be conducive to bringing new little Vancouverites into the world.) It seems that Vancouverites are more concerned with luxury items for dogs and fancy lobbies for high rise one bedrooms, than with the daily challenges of decent family housing for those in our workforce. Let us all think about what we are really saying to the hardworking men and women of our region who make a family income of less that $100,000, when we concern ourselves with the design lessons of fancy resorts, the latest in luxury dog treatments, and tax benefits for those who own $850,000 homes.

Think about it the next time you are helped by a policeman, a fireman, a teacher, a medical worker, or the nice woman who pours your coffee for $9.50 per hour.

Think about whether we should be studying resort lobbies or affordable housing programs.

Postscript: Since I wrote this chapter, Mr. Geller has returned to Vancouver and has, admirably, adjusted his interests to the problem of affordable housing. He is raising the issue of affordability now when he speaks, and in fact has become a candidate for the 2008 City Council elections. I am not sure whether it is a bad thing or a good thing that he is running for the NPA, but we shall hope for the best, and hope Vancouver and the Province have not spent so much during the good years that they will have nothing left for affordable housing in the challenging times ahead.

Chapter 7

The Lotos Doesn't Grow on Trees:
Gangs and the Distribution System

"6'n the morning' police at my door
Fresh adidas squeak across the bathroom floor
Out the back window I make a escape
Don't even get a chance to grab my old school tape

Mad with no music but happy 'cause I'm free
And the streets to a player is the place to be
Gotta knot in my pocket weighin' at least a grand
Gold on my neck my pistols close at hand

I'm a self made monster of the city streets
Remotely controlled by hard hip hop beats
But just livin' in the city is a serious task
Didn't know what the cops wanted
Didn't have the time to ask"

Ice-T, "6 'n the Morning", *Rhyme Pays*

Tennyson's "life of toil", to which Adam and Eve were sentenced after partaking of the forbidden fruit, implies a life of *honest* toil   When I grew up in small town Southern Ontario, I believe that the culture valued "an honest day's work".

In the days before factories started closing and the public sector unions began to dominate organized labour in Canada, there were lots of manufacturing companies, with union members belonging to the Teamsters, the Steelworkers, the UAW, the IBEW, etc., etc.

Where I grew up, there were a few large factories dominating the economy, and they were all unionized.   Labour Day, the day before we headed back to school after summer break, meant going downtown to watch the Labour Day parade. There were the floats, the marching bands and the clowns. But what I remember the best, is the rows of men and women marching with their union locals, proudly wearing their little caps with the local unit number of the union, embroidered on the cap.

Moreover, I remember all the applause for these men and women as they walked proudly down the street. It made a big impression on me. So great an impression, that in the future, I would become a real estate developer concentrating on affordable rental housing for lower income working people. (Not so much for the unionized workers, but mostly for non-union fast food and other service workers making $8 to $12 per hour.) I never forgot the lesson that working people are deserving of respect.

Somewhere along the line, however, our culture changed. The culture now seems to give its highest regard to fast money, easy money, and anyone who laboured away for years at a low-paying job is not given a lot of respect in our cultural milieu.   Our media has become full of stories of how real estate fortunes are made in a few years, and how perceptive stock pickers make millions in the stock market. The high tech revolution brought with it the "dot.com" millionaires, often still in their 20s.   The cult of celebrity worship misled thousands of impressionable young people that the right break in music or film could translate into millions of dollars in a short time frame.

Late night television is full of advertorials for courses teaching how to make a million in real estate, and how to "flip" properties.   There is even a television network about housing that offers up fare showing Joe Average how he too can learn to spot undervalued houses, do some quick renovations, and turn over the property for fast profit.

New condo projects in Greater Vancouver feature an "advance showing" for investors and friends of the developer, so within 24 hours of the units being shown to outside buyers, they are sold out. Fast money comes when the building is almost finished two years later and the insiders can sell out their units for $50,000 profit per unit.

The real estate listings are full of "assignments" being the polite term for this cashing out by the speculators, on the backs of the working people, who will now buy the units at the higher cost.

And nowhere in Canada comes close to Vancouver in the number of fraudulent stock 'promoters" and other investment "counselors" who are ready to help the foolish part with their hard-earned money, as we shall see in more detail in Chapter 10.

Nowhere in Canada is it as hard to figure out just what it is that some people are doing to support their lavish lifestyles than in Vancouver. Combining this cultural prevalence of fast money from vague sources with the astronomical cost of housing, it is little wonder that the young, the disaffected, and the dishonest are attracted to drug trafficking in Vancouver and the Lower Mainland.

In *Vancouver* magazine's December 2007 list of the fifty most powerful people in Vancouver, number seven was John Bryce, president of the East End chapter of the Hell's Angels (one of the richest and most powerful chapters of one of the most powerful gangs in Canada).

Moreover, in the land of the lotus, drugs are not stigmatized the same way they are in much of the rest of North America. For if Mom and Dad were West Coast hippies in the late 60s, and smoked dope and dropped acid, then why is there any stigma against taking drugs? And somebody has to manufacture/grow, distribute and market this component of the Lotos.

Nowhere in Canada is there more ambivalence in the culture towards the issue of drugs, both recreational and hard-core. On my walks with my dog through my neighbourhood of Kitsilano in the evening, it is very common to smell the marijuana smoke. In a city of environmentalists warning of the evils of every other kind of smoke, curiously the marijuana smoke is regarded with sympathetic diffidence.

This was driven home to me when attending a concert by Bob Dylan. Before he even appeared on the stage, the air was thick with clouds of marijuana smoke. There were two young women seated in front of me, and one was enjoying her marijuana "joint". Then, her friend, reached into her purse, and pulled out a package of cigarettes, and began to light one. The former, the one with the joint, got all upset, and yelled, "Don't you know that there is no smoking allowed in here?"

To be sure, the harder drugs, the one that create such horrible addictions are viewed differently. Yet here again, there is a different standard from the rest of the country, and we shall explore the ideology of the Downtown Eastside in Chapter 8.

However, it is easy to understand that in the land of the Lotos, which also happens to be the land of fast money, there is a cultural background for drug trafficking and distribution unlike any in Canada.

And since the late '80s, we have Canadian young men listening to something called "Gangsta Rap", a sub-genre of Hip Hop and Rap Music, which can be said to glorify the gangster life of black drug dealers, pimps and other criminals in American inner cities. It is one thing for young black men in tough American cities to listen to this fountain of anger, homophobia, misogynism, and promotion of gang life and street hustling. It is quite another for a wide group of Canadians, including Indo-Canadian and Vietnamese second generation kids in Surrey, to adopt the music and cultural icons as their own. While plenty of pop songs, starting in the mid '60s have flirted with the promotion of "getting high", there was always a cheerful innocence about the songs, a quiet reach towards the Lotos, if you will. But Gangsta Rap transcended the "simple" pleasures of a "joint", to romanticize the criminal life of the gangs distributing both drugs and prostitutes – an attractive proposition to young men looking for fast and "easy" money in a culture idolizing those who have achieved success fast and easy.

Whatever the cultural milieu, however, the fact is that drugs are a big business, and an illegal business; and whenever those two factors are present, so is organized crime. Inevitably, the brutal business organizations called "gangs", become part of a violent and lucrative form of organized crime "corporate take over", which, instead of using lawyers and accountants, uses shootings and murders.

While most of the drug distribution is done by gangs, there are plenty of reports of small operators getting caught, with their "grow-ops" cultivating marijuana in residential houses, or with a load of drugs buried under more legitimate freight by a trucker in a large tractor-trailer, or in one case with a cute plan involving a small building right by the American border.   In the last mentioned case, a couple of fellows bought a small building fronting on a small road along the American border south of Vancouver. They then set about excavating a tunnel under the road, under the border, with the idea of delivering drugs through the tunnel to the American side.   Unfortunately for them, the police discovered the plan, and were waiting to arrest them when finally they completed their laborious task and reached their destination on the American side of the border.

But most of the action is controlled by gangs. Periodically, the gangs undergo "competitive" rationalization of their marketplace and the assassinations and murders flare up, to the public's attention.   One such period in Vancouver was the time frame from August to November, 2007.   Here is what happened (summary based on articles from *The Vancouver Sun*, November 7, 2007):

- August 9, 2007: At 4:30 a.m. at an all-night Chinese restaurant on East Broadway, two masked gunmen burst shooting, killing two and injuring six. As is usual in these cases, the police stated that two of the victims were "known to police".
- September 6, 2007: A 27-year old man "known to police" was shot and his body dumped on the bank of the Fraser River in Richmond.
- September 8, 2007: At the Quattro restaurant on West 4th, masked gunmen fired through the glass window at Gurmit Singh Dhak, and a female, who both survived. Dhak is a well-known figure in gang circles, with various criminal charges and past experience having his Lexus fired at.

- September 11, 2007: As Len Pelletier (a Langley man with alleged Hells Angels links) was driving his son to school in his Hummer, pursuers shot several rounds at him after his Hummer crashed into a ditch during the chase.
- September 24, 2007: Jason Louie, a 34 year old club promoter "known to police" was shot dead in his Infinity SUV just off East Broadway.
- October 10, 2007: Dylan Krishna Becker, 38, is shot dead in Surrey.
- October 19, 2007: In an apartment in a Surrey condo tower, six people are shot dead in an execution style murder. Four are known gang members with criminal records pertaining to drug trafficking and weapons, but two, including a 55 year old gas fireplace repairman, appeared to have the misfortune of being in the wrong place at the wrong time.
- October 31, 2007: Vancouver police confirm that the shooting by a gunman of Hiep Quang Do, in a Vietnamese restaurant, was a targeted killing of someone "known to police".
- November 2, 2007: In his $5 million mansion in Shaughnessy, 45 year old Hong Chao (Raymond) Huang, a leader of the notorious Big Circle Boys Gang, is murdered. He is described as a major player in the Canadian drug trade.
- November 6, 2007: Ali Abhari, 25, a well-known Persian gangster and drug dealer, and Ronal Shakeel Raj, 31, a trucker who had links to the United Nations gang, were murdered in their Mercedes when they were cut off by two SUV's on a Vancouver city street. Raj, the "trucker" co-owns an $802,000 house and leased both a Cadillac Escalade and a Mercedes Benz.

As of the date of the most recent incident, Vancouver police had not made any arrests in any of the above crimes. Nor are they likely to in the future. A Statistics Canada study released in October, 2007 discloses that only 45% of gang-related killings in Canada in 2006 were solved by police, compared to 80% of non-gang homicides. In B.C., the figures are even more compelling, with police success on just 39% of gang related killings.

In his article in *The Vancouver Sun* on November 7, 2007, entitled, "Why gangsters get away with murder", *Sun* reporter Chad Skelton points out that witnesses who are gang members do not come forward to police, and witnesses who are not gang members are too frightened to come forward to police. Skelton provides statistics that in fact there has been no overall increase in the number of gang-related killings. He quotes criminologist Yvon Dandurand as saying that gang killings only appear to be on the increase, because they typically come in "spurts, a cycle of payback and retribution that can take a while to calm down". Says Dandurand: "If you're a criminal organization and someone shoots one of your guys, there's no way you can leave that unpunished. If there's one gang assassination, (police) start preparing for the next one."

So why do gang-related murders create banner headlines on the front pages of the local newspapers, *The Vancouver Sun* and *The Province*? Why do the citizens demand police action every time gangsters kill other gangsters? I think there are several reasons:

Firstly, there is the quite legitimate fear, that shootings in restaurants, on a public street, or in an apartment building can injure or kill innocent people. This same fear came to the forefront in Toronto a couple of years ago when a teenage girl, shopping on Yonge Street, was hit and killed by a stray bullet in a gang shoot-out.

But, secondly, the gang warfare strikes at the heart of the myth in Vancouverism that drug trafficking is more or less a victimless crime. If the addicts can take the drugs in the Insite facility, and we don't have to think too much about the distribution system, then the Lotus Land can continue to soft-pedal the moral morass that is the drug culture of the West Coast.

Thirdly, we recognize that there are insufficient police to handle the problem. In 2005, Vancouver police admitted, that with existing staff, they were only able to investigate less than 30 per cent of the criminal groups in the province. In a recent report commissioned by Vancouver City Hall concerning the size of the local police force, it was recommended that an additional 129 officers were needed. Council eventually approved just 17 new officers.

As the City blames senior levels of government regarding funding transfers, the average citizen knows very well that it is hard to recruit and retain police officers whose salaries are insufficient to support their families in the hot real estate market of Lotus Land. New recruits will not keep pace with retirements and attrition, as existing officers move away to other cities where they can afford to live somewhere near their work, so that after an all-night shift they don't have to drive for 2 hours to get to their affordable homes.
Fourthly, there is an understanding that the answer to drug related violence is the same as the answer was to Prohibition era rum-running gangsters. If the Government would step in, and take control of the drug distribution system, and administer the drugs in the therapeutic model that I discuss in Chapter 8, then many of the gangs would lose their raison d'etre.

In the meantime, we are relying on American authorities to catch B.C. gang members as they supply the American market. For example, Clayton Roueche, the boss of the Fraser Valley-based UN gang, was arrested in early June, 2008 in the U.S. and was denied bail in Oklahoma.

Knowing that Lotus Land has created the drug distribution system of the gangs, that drug use itself is out of control, that there is little success in solving gang-related crime, and that Lotus Land has created a real estate market where policemen cannot afford housing, all makes people very uneasy - which comes out as a cry for police to take care of the problem of the public executions on our streets.

In contemporary culture, we all want to blame someone else for every problem. With respect to gangs, the police blame the court system, the court system blames the education system, the media blame the police, the police blame the immigration system, etc., etc.

But as the great cartoonist Walt Kelly, in his *Pogo* comic strip, once said, *"We have met the enemy and he is us."* Kelly was actually referring to the problem of pollution, but the same can be said for many of our contemporary problems, and I would suggest that in Lotus Land, we admit, "We have met the enemy and he is the Lotos-Eater, himself."

We explore in greater depth the relationship of Lotus Land to drugs in the next chapter. Before we do so, there is an interesting, but little discussed, connection between the drug trade and the lack of affordable housing in Vancouver.

For one thing, we realize that drug money is being "laundered" through the purchase of condos, thereby creating additional demand and pushing up prices.   For another, there is an artificial, non-residential, demand for rental housing, which is removing these houses from the real market for families needing rental housing.   That is because Vancouver has a huge industry of "grow-ops", where marijuana is being grown indoors.

Carlito Pablo, writing in the *Georgia Straight* on January 24, 2008, quotes Carlene Robbins, manager of Vancouver's property-use branch as saying, "A lot of the grow-ops, the majority of the grow-ops that we bust, are in residential buildings, most of them single-family (houses) and many of them are rental. Basically, they're not being used for living. They're being used to grow marijuana, so there is an impact (on the supply of rental housing)"
Pablo's article discloses that Vancouver has been closing on average some 500 grow-ops per year, Surrey has been busting over 200 per year, with Richmond has been taking down some one or two a week.

Most experts believe that the province has between 10,000 and 20,000 indoor cannabis-growing operations.   The RCMP pegs the annual marijuana trade in B.C. at some $7 *billion* dollars per year, making it a major component of the province's economy.

For a working family in Lotus Land, the competition for housing with the Lotos indoor cultivators, is yet another insult to honest, hard working people as they go about their lives seeking a dignified place to live.

Chapter 8

The Downtown Eastside:
Through the Looking Glass

"How would you like to live in Looking-glass House, Kitty? I wonder if they'd give you milk in there? Perhaps Looking-glass milk isn't good to drink--But oh, Kitty! now we come to the passage. You can just see a little PEEP of the passage in Looking-glass House, if you leave the door of our drawing-room wide open: and it's very like our passage as far as you can see, only you know it may be quite different on beyond."

Lewis Carroll, *Through the Looking Glass*

"But I don't want to go among mad people," Alice remarked.
"Oh, you can't help that," said the Cat: "we're all mad here. I'm mad. You're mad."
"How do you know I'm mad?" said Alice.
"You must be," said the Cat, "or you wouldn't have come here."
Alice didn't think that proved it at all; however, she went on. " And how do you know that you're mad?"
"To begin with," said the Cat, "a dog's not mad. You grant that?"
"I suppose so," said Alice.
"Well, then," the Cat went on, "you see, a dog growls when it's angry, and wags its tail when it's pleased. Now I growl when I'm pleased, and wag my tail when I'm angry. Therefore I'm mad."

Lewis Carroll, *Alice in Wonderland*

"Though you might hear laughin', spinnin', swingin' madly across the sun,
It's not aimed at anyone, it's just escapin' on the run
And but for the sky there are no fences facin'.

89

And if you hear vague traces of skippin' reels of rhyme
To your tambourine in time, it's just a ragged clown behind,
I wouldn't pay it any mind, it's just a shadow you're
Seein' that he's chasing.

Hey! Mr. Tambourine Man, play a song for me,
I'm not sleepy and there is no place I'm going to.
Hey! Mr. Tambourine Man, play a song for me,
In the jingle jangle morning I'll come followin' you.

Then take me disappearin' through the smoke rings of my mind,
Down the foggy ruins of time, far past the frozen leaves,
The haunted, frightened trees, out to the windy beach,
Far from the twisted reach of crazy sorrow.
Yes, to dance beneath the diamond sky with one hand waving free,
Silhouetted by the sea, circled by the circus sands,
With all memory and fate driven deep beneath the waves,
Let me forget about today until tomorrow.

Hey! Mr. Tambourine Man, play a song for me,
I'm not sleepy and there is no place I'm going to.
Hey! Mr. Tambourine Man, play a song for me,
In the jingle jangle morning I'll come followin' you."

Bob Dylan, "Mr. Tambourine Man", from the album, *Bringing it all Back Home*

Our policy towards the drug-addicted and the mentally ill of the Downtown Eastside suffers from the ideological confusion evidenced by the Judge in the Ellison case, discussed in Chapter 3. After a two week trial exposing a "monstrous breach of trust", the Judge gave a sentence of two years' house (or was it boat?) arrest. The lack of severity of the sentence did not accord with the severity of the words. It is an old story that words are one thing, and actions are another. Even a short jail sentence in Ellison's case would have *shown* how

90

seriously we regard teachers abusing their trust by sexually taking advantage of their students – the Court could have shown how strongly we as a society *denounce* the behaviour. That it did not do so, leaves all with the impression, correct or not, that in Vancouver such conduct is not all that serious.

Why do we return to Ellison in a discussion of the Downtown Eastside? It is my contention, that the Downtown Eastside (DES) is in fact the Lotus Land "through the looking glass". What the DES teaches us, is a lot more *about us* than about the pathetic, damaged people who inhabit that nightmare 4 square blocks within "the best place on earth".

The fact that we see nothing wrong with the values of the Lotus Land, means that we cannot strongly denounce the underside of the Lotus Land. For if Vancouver, accepts, even welcomes, the various types of addiction to the Lotos, then it cannot denounce those whose personalities are so marginal that their addictions become all-encompassing.

If Vancouverites are the mariners of Tennyson's poem, and accept the values of these mariners, we must accept that the winners and losers in Lotus Land will look a little different than in the rest of Canada. The winners will be those who have homes with the best of the water-views, make the maximum income with the minimum of hard toil, and have the best toys and the best wine. The losers will be those who have no homes at all, be reduced to scavenging for bottles and cans that can be sold to recycling depots, and have the cheapest wine, and the hardest drugs to escape their cognizance of what "losers" they are.

Tennyson's mariners, as we discussed in Chapter 5, even state that "death" might be preferable to a life of toil. This indeed is one of the ideological underpinnings of the apparent death-wish of the life of addiction to hard drugs in the Downtown Eastside.

How can we *denounce* the flip side of who we are, and what we see by going through the looking glasses or mirrors of our own reflections? And so, we assuage our guilt by preventing these addicts from dying in the alleyways and allow them to shoot up in the supervised injection centre, called "Insite". Of course, I agree it is more humane, when we have nurses who can monitor cases of overdose, and call the ambulance so the addict will not die. Of course, I agree that there is some *therapeutic* rationale for having all the addicted and mentally ill in a four block section, or nightmarish theme park, where all the services we choose to give to them will be readily accessible.

But the fact that we have chosen not to give them hospital beds, not to re-open psychiatric beds which were closed by tight-fisted politicians, says more to me than any supervised injection site could ever say.

Most of these people are *mentally ill.* It is our choice whether to treat them or not. Making their drug injection experience safer is nice, but misses the point. They are the *casualties*, they are the *losers* of the Lotus land experience, and all of us, all the mariners who enjoy the positive side of that experience, have a moral obligation to look after the casualties, the mentally ill - just like we should look after the physically ill in our health care system. Give them drugs if necessary, but only under doctors' supervision in a psychiatric facility, that treats all the mental and physical illnesses of these folks. Allowing them to take the drugs in Insite, then closing our eyes to what activities must be undertaken by them to afford the drugs, and closing our eyes to the broken people sleeping in the woods in Stanley Park, is an embarrassment to a City where people have no problem paying $700,000 for a two-bedroom condo with a view.

There are a substantial group of people in the Downtown Eastside who are included in the term, "hard to house". The wonderful Portland Hotel Society, an organization with a "no eviction" policy understands that for the mentally ill, addicted, personality disordered occupants, a reflexive policy of adaption to the needs of these unfortunates is more appropriate for them than the typical model of evictions and revolving homelessness for these, the most wounded of our society. (For more information on the Portland Hotel Society, refer to the study by Penny Gurstein and Dan Small in *Housing Studies,* Vol. 20, Number 5, p. 717.)

By February, 2008, the Vancouver Police Department released a report that made clear that Vancouver was trying to offload onto the police the job of dealing with the mentally ill that should be done by medical facilities.   The report was called *Lost in Transition* and vividly subtitled *How a Lack of Capacity in the Mental Health System is Failing Vancouver's Mentally Ill and Draining Police Resources.*

Apparently, some one-third of Vancouver police service calls, city-wide, deal with the mentally ill, and this increases to one-half in the Downtown Eastside.   To give an indication of the extent of the problem, the Vancouver police report states that in 1999, it made some 360 arrests under the provisions of the B.C. Mental Health Act (which direct the police to arrest someone deemed to be a danger to either himself or others).   But by 2007, this number had mushroomed to 1,743.

Lack of long-term care and hospital space are perhaps well-known causes of the problem of so many mentally-ill people on our streets. But the VPD report criticizes as well the lack of resources for people suffering what is called the "concurrent disorder" of both mental health and addictions problems.   The report criticizes the common practice of mental health clinics to require those with concurrent disorders to first "sober" up, (or get addictions counseling) and only then qualify for mental health treatment.

Too many of those with the dual disorders then, remain untreated, living on the streets of the Downtown Eastside, and the job of dealing with them is dumped on to the police.   The provincial government, in the wake of this report, is starting to make some promises about new institutional beds (in June of 2008, it announced a new 100 bed facility in Burnaby), but the fact that the situation was allowed to get this bad, speaks volumes about the tolerance for what should be intolerable.

There is a study underway called NAOMI – North American Opiate Medication Initiative.   This is a controlled clinical trial for opiate injection users who have failed to respond to other treatments, with centres in both Vancouver and Montreal.   Some users are given methadone, some heroin, and some hydromorphine, which is pharmaceutically similar to heroin. The program is controversial; an editorial in the June 2006 edition of *Canadian Family Physician* argued for a number of reasons that it would be more prudent to simply extend methadone treatment by community-based family physicians. In any event, there are a number of reasons why it is insufficient to simply have the supervised injection site, which exists in the DES, where addicts are monitored as they inject themselves, and the supervisors can call ambulances for any of the addicts who overdose.

While Insite certainly prevents deaths in back alleys, it is hardly a substitute for a more complete therapeutic treatment style for the often mentally ill addicts, who also are plagued with high incidence of HIV and Hepatitis C infection.   To see the wasted lives of the DES, is to wonder about the tolerance of Vancouverites for what is happening – is the only concern that we don't want to see dead bodies in the alleys? What about the damage done to mentally ill people using injection drugs? What about the cost of the drugs?   What about the crime necessary to support the habits?   What about the fact that drug trafficking at its source enriches the horrible Taliban in Afghanistan and the criminal state of North Korea, which uses its drug profits to fund Weapons of Mass Destruction, (which it is now starting to export to such terrorist supporting states as Syria).

An article in *The Vancouver Sun* on September 9, 2008, reported that the methadone treatments for heroin addiction now amount to a $27 million a year industry for B.C. pharmacies. And, unsurprisingly, in Lotus Land, the article cited concerns that some pharmacies are offering cash kickbacks to their patients in return for filling the prescriptions and being able to bill Pharmacare $8.60 for dispensing a daily dose of methadone and an extra $7.70 to supervise the patient while he or she takes the dose. Drugs are big business indeed.

The Downtown Eastside is a horrible plague upon the Lotus Land; it requires massive amounts of government money to treat the addicted mentally ill.   The fact that the wealthy in Lotus Land are not *demanding* these programs, cast doubt upon the moral standards and commitment to social justice and health care by the Lotos-Eaters.

Fortunately, the Province of British Columbia did make one wise decision by buying approximately a dozen of the "single-room occupancy" hotels in the DES catering to the poor and addicted. There was a real fear that they would be lost to neglect and then redevelopment. The Province has a budget for fixing them up, to reach a certain basic standard of livability.　But, in the absence of new affordable rental housing (because of the absence of inducement programs to the private sector – which programs exist in other areas of Canada and the United States), these rooms will start to be taken by low income downtown service workers.　That is because a service worker in the Downtown making just over minimum wage cannot afford to live anywhere close to Downtown.　For those without vehicles and the unwillingness to ride transit for hours every day, they are starting to rent the housing which in the past was only suitable for welfare recipients, leaving the addicted and mentally ill back homeless on the street.

Another recent announcement of promise is the December, 2007 announcement of joint Provincial-Municipal action to develop 12 municipally owned housing sites for social housing, including that for tenants with mental health issues.　This is discussed more in the next chapter.

I do have a fear that gentrification and redevelopment will start to eat away at the DES.　When that happens, there is the danger that the mentally ill and addicted will be dispersed through Metro Vancouver, which will make it harder to treat them with the limited programs now available.　At least, they are now visible, and therefore easier to help. I worry when I read businesspeople and developers talk about developing the area.　I worry that having a "theme park" for the drug addicted and mentally ill will be seen as detrimental to Vancouver's all important "image" to the world as we host the Winter Olympics. Dispersing these people will not solve the problem - just the contrary as it will make it harder for existing programs to treat them.　Having the problem "visible" is important to stirring up the moral imperatives to help treat the wasted humans of the DES.

Gentrification and re-development has already started. The City's 2005 Downtown Eastside housing plan aimed to stabilize the 10,000 units of low-income housing which have been available for decades, and then "add" 4000 units of market housing. But by 2008, there were already 1750 market units in planning or under construction. The process is driven by the imperatives of development when the rest of Downtown Vancouver has already been built up. As Vancouver developer Michael Geller pointed out in a *Vancouver Sun* story of May 3, 2008: "The land down here (the Downtown Eastside) is currently selling for more than prime sites in Burnaby."

Because of the lack of attention to the future of the Downtown Eastside by our politicians, some concerned citizens, including highly-respected businessman Milton Wong, decided to form their own committee, called the Downtown Eastside Community Land Use Principles project (Declup). They are striving to determine how new market development can co-exist with enhanced housing and supports for the low-income, addicted and mentally ill, who depend on the DES. We wish them well in their efforts.

We worry, however, about the mainstream politicians and citizens of Vancouver who seem to care so little about the DES. We worry that in an age where the only value that the politically correct can publicly articulate is "tolerance", then everything is tolerable. The first step in solving society's problems is to admit that they are *our* problems too, the second to *denounce* them as problems, the third to take *action* to solve them, and the fourth is to understand that it may cost *us* something to fix, and that we cannot simply pass along the costs to future residents, through ever more onerous obligations in development agreements, resulting in ever higher cost of housing to future residents.

Just like in sentencing, rehabilitation, deterrence and protection of the public are important, but so is *denunciation.* We must denounce the twisted values of our "underclass", even as we treat the psychiatric and physiological results of such values. It is too easy to pretend that they are just "victims" of a social determinism that absolves them from the obvious effects of their irresponsible behaviours. It is too easy to pretend that their sicknesses have nothing to do with us. Accordingly, first we must admit that their values, their running from the assumption of personal responsibility, too often mirror what they see amongst the "winners" of Lotus Land.

If, to the mariners, there is no value in life higher than pleasure, then we have a built-in time-bomb for our civilization: firstly, don't bother having children, because they interfere with the parents' pursuit of pleasure; secondly, if you *do* have children, see your children only as appendages of the narcissistic parents, guaranteeing their alienation from you; thirdly, in teaching that life is about the pursuit of pleasure, you guarantee that if your children are wealthy enough to have so much of every earthly pleasure, to the point of boredom, then drugs will be the only pleasure left to pursue (just think of the rock stars and actors who, despite their financial abilities to have a life of pleasure, eventually self-destruct this way).

It seems that a life of addiction results either from running away from the *pain* of a tragic life (which so many of the DES addicts have had), or from the *boredom* of a life that is sated with pleasure, but lacks other foundational values, that give meaning to a life of toil, a life of doing good in the world. So too many in Vancouver's mainstream, descended from the Lotos Eaters, are addicts in one way or another, because they cannot derive pleasure anymore from the simple pleasures of family life, work, and community. And so, in Lotus Land, the underclass and the upper class are fundamentally linked

The horrible waste of lives in the drug-trafficking world of the gangs, discussed in Chapter 7, could be lessened by legally dispensing drugs within the context of a psychiatric facility, or by community-based physicians. And for the "soft drugs" like marijuana, we must ultimately make the determination whether these drugs have more in common with alcoholic beverages and hence should be legalized and sold in liquor stores (and hence cut out the illegal distribution networks of the gangs) or must continue to be denounced as similar to harder drugs.

How do we expect the addicts to pay for the cost of their drugs? According to Vancouver Police, (in a story by Gerry Bellett in the June 24, 2008 edition of the *Vancouver Sun*) Vancouver is only city in the world with "chronic offender syndrome" where criminals with more than 100 theft convictions are returned to the street shortly after each conviction. These are older drug addicts who commit theft to buy crack cocaine. How do we expect the police and the courts to deal with this problem? Why do we foist this problem on the people who are victimized by this crime? The Police, naturally, call for longer sentences. The Courts, as we shall see below, are tired of having to use the criminal law to battle a problem that Vancouver's society should address in a comprehensive fashion, and refuse to accede to the understandable position of the police to get chronic criminals off the street. And so, we must conclude that there is something basically wrong in our system for dealing with the addicted who do not let the laws stand in the way of their need to feed their addictions.

Vancouver Police want to stop the minor sentences once a chronic offender hits 30 convictions - at which time the law would mandate a federal prison term (automatic for sentences of two years or more) so that the offender could receive treatment for drug addiction at a federal institution. This is an understandable position.

There are some others who are moving in the right direction. With respect to a model of treatment, the fact that the mentally ill and addicted of the DES are basically within a four-block area, is what makes it possible to treat them, under the present regime of inadequate psychiatric beds. In other words, if we will not pay to bring the mentally ill into our hospitals, then we must go to them. This is the model that originated in the 1960s in Madison, Wisconsin, called Assertive Community Treatment: A team of 10 to 12 health professionals, including a psychiatrist, psychologist, nurses and social workers, each with a caseload of a dozen patients, is responsible to seek out its patients and treat them where they are. Recently, the respected Portland Hotel Society of the Downtown Eastside, which houses and treats some of the most difficult residents there, together with Vancouver Coastal Health, have adopted a roaming health team, under the leadership of psychiatrist Dr. Bill MacEwan, with three nurses and a social worker.

The crucial feature of this model, according to Liz Evans, founder of the Portland Hotel Society, is that they get to know the patients. Dr. MacEwan, not only roams through the DES seeing patients where they live, three days a week, but he also works at White Rock's Peace Arch Hospital and both St. Paul's Hospital and UBC Hospital in Vancouver. There was an excellent profile of Dr. MacEwan and his work in the December 2007 *Vancouver* magazine. MacEwan notes that many drug addicted, mentally ill patients have revolving admissions to hospital to treat not only their mental illnesses, but the various "ricochet effects" of a life as a drug addict on the street – HIV, Hepatitis C, and infections like pneumonia. He came to realize that even with the tremendous expenses of treating such people in the hospital, they are discharged back into the situation which contributes to their illnesses and thus, he says, "we're leaving the most severely ill on their own." The professional reason he does his work in the way he does is that it makes more sense to go and find the people in distress than to wait for them to come to the hospital. Getting to know the patients as individuals is key, because they are in fact very complex and difficult, sometimes abusive, patients.

Dr. MacEwan does not frame his work in spiritual terms. He says simply that for a physician like himself, who has the opportunity to help, "how can you turn your back?" Unfortunately Dr. MacEwan's program is the exception rather than the rule.

And we are reminded of the futility of trying to use the blunt weapon of the criminal justice system to deal with out-of-control repeat offenders with substance abuse and mental health issues. Recently, the British Columbia Court of Appeal made a plea to the British Columbia government, which was covered in Ian Mulgrew's November 26, 2007 column in *The Vancouver Sun*. In this decision, the Justices concluded a lower court judge had difficulty sentencing a 27-year-old repeat offender, because there was no medical help available. Mulgrew quotes Justice Catherine Anne Ryan: "This Court can do no more than to acknowledge the lack of resources and urge our legislators to respond to the need." The Court acknowledged that it is being asked to deal with offenders whose probation orders are meaningless without the availability of treatment services. Without helping the offender to deal with the underlying psychological problems, it is likely that he or she will re-offend upon release.

Says Mulgrew: "More jail time – the solution some propose – doesn't help this population, in my view, because they're not bent, they're broken. These people are not making criminal choices, they're out of control."

And so, somewhere along the line, we must stand up and say the mariners were wrong for saying there is no pleasure in fighting evil. We must stand up and say that there is pleasure in doing the right thing, and we must establish additional agreed-upon values, other than just tolerance. When that happens, I hope that the idea of paying higher taxes to support more Dr. MacEwans, and more full-scale treatment facilities and psychiatric hospitals, including those geared to helping those clogging up our criminal justice system, will become a value of Vancouverism, just as is paying higher taxes to hire and properly remunerate more police officers.

Until that time, we must understand that a society that glamorizes a Britney Spears or a Paris Hilton, and that pretends there are no values other than tolerance, and no ideology other than finding someone to blame, creates the underclass it deserves. We must join Dr. MacEwan in refusing to turn our backs on what is just "through the looking glass".

By not having a policy of inducing the construction of modest rental housing for lower income working people, who have assumed the responsibilities of work, and providing for families, we show the underclass that there is no point in working. By neglecting our low income working class, we make a statement that is all too well understood. By having our well educated and upper income people, living lives of addiction and promiscuity, and pursuing tattoos instead of religion, celebrating a Paris Hilton and mocking those with "traditional" values in politics as "right wing fundamentalists", we pass a serious message through the looking glass.

Theodore Dalrymple is a British psychiatrist and writer working in the psychiatric ward of a British slum hospital as well as a nearby prison. He has written an important book, *Life at the Bottom: The Worldview That Makes the Underclass* (Ivan Dee). His book argues that poverty isn't caused by economics, but rather by a wildly dysfunctional --- and rapidly spreading --- set of values. A blindly forgiving welfare state in which being "nonjudgmental" is the highest objective has helped create a permanent, irredeemable class of victims, morally adrift and ineducable.

Dalrymple, who has worked with more than 10,000 such patients over many years' work as a psychiatrist is unafraid to link the misery of the underclass to misguided values, and a failure to take responsibility for their actions or inaction.

To those who have witnessed the roving bands of drunken youth on Granville Street in Downtown Vancouver on a Saturday night, Dalrymple's description of British youth should be interesting: "To reach Saturday night is the summit of ambition of much of English youth," he writes. "Nothing fills their minds with such anticipation or eagerness. No career, no pastime, no interest, can compete with the joys of Saturday night, when the center of the city turns into a B-movie Sodom and Gomorrah,"

If the culture of our elites has turned into a quest for the latest "victims", then the dysfunctionality of the DES underclass is in fact reinforced by our elites viewing them through ideological victimology. In other words, the culture of Lotus Land does its best to persuade the members of the DES underclass that they have no responsibility for their own actions and are not the molders of their own lives.

If the present day elites of Lotus Land spent many years following "Mr. Tambourine Man" and cannot or will not toil away at supporting "values", then the weakest denizens of Lotus Land will fall Through the Looking Glass;   we are responsible because we have created them;

and we are responsible to educate ourselves as well as them that without Responsibility, all of Vancouver can fall Through the Looking Glass.

I conclude this chapter with a plot summary of a little known Canadian film called "The Lotus Eaters", that I came across while researching this book. The 1993 movie is about a family in a small community on one of the Gulf Islands off Vancouver in the 1960s as the "enlightenment" of the hippie era enters their lives. This summary is by Clarke Fountain of *All Movie Guide:*

"It is the 1960s, but Hal Kingswood (R.H. Thomson), the old-fashioned headmaster of a small school in British Colombia not far from Vancouver hasn't quite gotten hip to it yet. He won't even let his late-teen daughter Cleo (Tara Frederick) go to a concert alone with her boyfriend Dwayne (Gabe Khouth). Zoe (Aloka McLean) is Hal's youngest daughter, full of romantic ideas and idealistic notions, and she narrates most of this domestic drama. At school, a beloved teacher suddenly dies, and she is replaced by Anne-Marie Andrews (Michele-Barbara Pelletier), a stylish and charismatic younger woman from Quebec who immediately inspires Zoe to feats of imitation. However, Zoe is horrified to discover that she is not the only one who finds Anne-Marie inspiring: her father Hal is having an affair with her. This all comes to light when the family is together celebrating Christmas, and for a time it looks like everyone will split up. It doesn't help the family much when Cleo has announces that she is pregnant and isn't interested in participating in the outmoded institution of marriage."

And so, we finally understand that whether we are talking about Tennyson's "The Lotos-Eaters' or a minor Canadian movie called "The Lotus Eaters", the embrace of the lotus fruit and the lotus values by Vancouver's middle classes, starting in the late '60s, had a variety of consequences; when that embrace of the lotus passed to the underclass, "Mr. Tambourine Man" morphed into the "Mr. Dissipated Man" now populating that dreadful place Through the Looking Glass. Bob Dylan's narrator in "Mr. Tambourine Man" says that, having tired of chasing his shadow, he is ready to take the journey "through the smoke rings of (his) mind", because he is not sleepy and *"there is no place (he's) going to."*

We, in Vancouver, had better figure out a place worth "going to", that offers more than *beauty* and more than *pleasure,* and more than what Mr. Tambourine Man offers:

"Yes, to dance beneath the diamond sky with one hand waving free, Silhouetted by the sea, circled by the circus sands, With all memory and fate driven deep beneath the waves, Let me forget about today until tomorrow."

It is time to clearly denounce the hippie/mariner tradition in Vancouver's culture.

Chapter 9

EcoDensity and the Fraud on the Young

"Nowadays in Vancouver, if like me you are middle aged and own your digs, it can seem cruel to invite younger adults over for dinner, a taunt to those whose incomes are relentlessly outstripped by real estate inflation. Even worse, you begin to sense that you and your guests are on opposite sides of a firming up political divide. You are, after all, a member of the generation that is asking the young to endure and solve global warming, but what have you done for them lately, besides pouring fine wines in a heritage home of the sort they can never aspire to have?"

David Beers, "Vancouver Eats Its Young", *The Tyee* (www.thetyee.ca,) October 23, 2007

"And sweet it was to dream of Fatherland,
Of child, and wife, and slave; but evermore
Most weary seem'd the sea, weary the oar,
Weary the wandering fields of barren foam.
Then some one said, 'We will return no more';"

Alfred Tennyson, "The Lotos-Eaters"

Although we have been discussing the cultural foundations of the problems of the Downtown Eastside, there are concrete political causes for the problem, attributable to every level of government. The homelessness problem of the Downtown Eastside is, in part, related to Federal and Provincial policies. When the Federal government cut certain transfer payments to the provinces and the provinces then cut welfare rates and rolls and cut the number of psychiatric beds, there was the predictable effect on homelessness.

Not so well understood, is the connection between the construction of new affordable rental housing and homelessness. Basically, when no new affordable units are created by the private sector development industry, because existing laws, programs and policies make it easier to make money from condos, then the entire low end housing market is affected.

As the Emperor in Chapter 2 concludes, there is no appetite in New City for affordable housing.   Vancouver does not wish to learn too much about affordable housing programs operating elsewhere, because, in fact, Vancouver does not really want affordable housing. As we shall see in this Chapter, Mayor Sam Sullivan's much-hyped "EcoDensity" program was initially more about environmental standards and the urban ecological footprint than it was about providing affordable housing for the population.   After two years of building the EcoDensity brand, ratepayers' reactions to the first draft of the program was to make it clear to the Mayor and the City's Planning Director, that the issue of affordability was being overlooked.

Clearly, a society that makes the welfare of its young a priority will emphasize the development of affordable rental *and* purchased housing, and emphasize housing that permits its occupants to reproduce and have space for their children to reside with them.   And a society that is truly serious about the environment will create housing for workers *throughout* the various parts of the city where they work, so that they will not have to drive for hours or take public transit for hours.

The development of thousands of small one bedrooms and expensive two bedrooms does nothing for those young people who are interested in family formation and child-rearing.

So, first of all, we ask why has Vancouver been developing itself this way?

One explanation is that the current high rise development represents a tried and true, certain, form of development that makes *good profits* for its developers. Developers like certainty. In a form of enterprise, which historically has been subject to the huge cyclical risks of economic booms and busts, the certainty of the Vancouver Model of development is a welcome change.

Another, is that Downtown Vancouver as urban playground, surrounded by the gorgeous seawall along the ocean, Stanley Park, and the clubs and restaurants, is a model that has been more appealing to Vancouverites than a model of mixed housing for various size families and various income groups. All those businesses oriented to the free-spending condo residents have created another disincentive to changing the population mix.

However, it is still amazing to me that the entire Vancouver Model has been so unwelcoming to all young people – not only those who wish to start families, and need bedroom space more than they need high end finishings, but also those just starting their careers who need something affordable somewhere close to where they work. And so we return to Tennyson's poem.

Tennyson's mariners, while acknowledging that it is "sweet" to dream of child (and wife), quickly conclude, (while sitting eating the Lotos fruit, and taking in the Lotos beauty as they sit down "upon the yellow sand, (b)etween the sun and moon upon the shore") that they will not return to Fatherland, wife or children. The mariners so quickly and without any pangs of conscience decide to abandon their children! They feel no obligations to their children; in fact, as narcissists, the only regard for their children, is the "sweetness" that thoughts of them give to the mariners themselves. What narcissists!

Abandoning all notions of good and evil, abandoning the notion of "toil" for the purpose of supporting a family, the mariners, self-centred druggies and esthetes that they are, see all of life through their Lotos-coloured glasses. Lacking empathy *for even their own children* they see no joy in anything but calm and beauty.

As Tennyson has his mariners say:

"Let us alone. Time driveth onward fast,
And in a little while our lips are dumb.
Let us alone. What is it that will last?
All things are taken from us, and become
Portions and parcels of the dreadful past."

Believing not in an afterlife, believing that nothing they can do with their lives will have a lasting effect on the future, they conclude that all things are to be taken from them and simply become part of a "dreadful past". This is such a depressing view, compared to those who live to "toil", live to create good in the world, live to create social justice, and live to repair the world and reestablish the paradise that was lost by Adam and Eve.

Instead of aspiring to the spiritual paradise of Adam and Eve, before their fall, the Lotos-Eaters accept a facsimile thereof. But the paradise of the Lotos is meant for slumber and calm only. Life is only viewed from the material viewpoint: after consumption of material things, such material things are gone, leaving only a dreadful past.

This approach to life of course, sees only that "Time driveth onward fast, (a)nd in a little while our lips are dumb." However, another approach might be to say that because time passes quickly, all the more reason for humankind to use the time wisely and create lasting good.

That other approach will say also that what lasts is what we create of lasting value. And one of the most important things we create is our own children. By teaching them well, and by installing in them good values, gives each of us a little bit of control over, a little contribution to, the future well-being of the world. But to *abandon* them to better enjoy our own experiences of beauty and the other goals of the Lotos, is to demonstrate a moral failing of the highest degree.

Furthermore, in common with most other areas of Canada, we ignore the crisis in the provision of quality and affordable day care. Young parents, already discouraged by the high cost of rent or mortgage, suffer through the lack of a decent day care system. On June 21st,

2008 the *Vancouver Sun*'s Chad Skelton did a brilliant expose of the dangers to children from the poor management and lack of resources of Greater Vancouver's day care facilities. By analyzing government inspection data, obtained under the Freedom of Information Act, Skelton found that daycares here had nearly 3000 "serious incidents", including 230 cases of children going "missing or wandering."

In a related article, Skelton posed the question of why day care inspection records are not publicly available (without going through the procedure under the Freedom of Information Act), while inspections of restaurants and tattoo parlours are freely available online. Tim Shum, regional manager of health protection for Fraser Health, was interviewed and stated that the matter is one of public demand.

Shum stated, "We looked at the area where we tend to get more questions from the general public. And we do get more questions from the public about restaurants than we do about child care."

And so, in Lotus Land, the mariners are much more interested in fine dining and safe tattoo parlours than fine and safe child care.

How demoralizing is it for young people to see that, in Vancouver, *pseudo*-environmentalism trumps affordability every time? How demoralizing is it for those in their early thirties seeing their parents enjoy "Freedom 55" (the brilliant marketing ploy of London Life Insurance) while they are signing on to 40 year amortization mortgages at the age of 35, thus delaying *their* "freedom" to 75? How demoralizing will it be for them to still be working hard to pay their mortgage debt in their 60s while their parents in their late 80s show no signs of slowing down, while those parents enjoy their wealth – which in many cases will have been created by buying cheap housing in the early 1970s and then selling it for millions 40 years later, a most unsustainable model?

And so, the Lotos-Eaters of Vancouver, who fail to plan for affordable housing for their children, are choosing one ideological position, and we must advocate a far different ideological position: in the process we must show the Lotos-Eaters what Tennyson shows to us, that they indeed have an ideological position, and it is not as nice as they think it is.

Let us look at the initial draft of Mayor Sam Sullivan's EcoDensity Charter.   Let us use it as an example of the mindset that simply ignores the problems of the young in buying a place in the Vancouver Model.

The first problem relates to the "recitals" of the document.   Legal documents often start with recitals, following the introductory word, "Whereas".   In this case, the Charter recites the problems that the Charter seek to address: the danger of climate change, environmental sustainability, the maintenance of livable neighbourhoods, and compact, mixed-use, walkable communities, looming environmental threats to these past achievements, the need to participate in global environmental efforts, and finally, the "opportunity to influence change, by using density, design, and land use to create more sustainable and affordable communities".

So the purpose of the document is said to mainly deal with environmental matters. Yet, there is a reference to "sustainable and affordable communities" achieved through "density, design and land use".   After a few more paragraphs setting out the City's commitment to "an over-arching environmental priority", a "green land use pattern", "greener design", "green and livable support systems", there is a section pledging to accommodate "density of different types and scales to meet a full range of housing needs, including singles, families, empty-nesters and seniors". This is followed by a pledge to use "density to enable greater housing affordability through a generally increased supply of more inherently affordable housing".

The document attempts to explain how density helps the environment, for example, through transportation and building energy use.   We cannot dispute that putting people close to shopping and public transit is environmentally desirable.

But how does the City explain that density, or at least its policy of EcoDensity, will help affordability?   Again, it claims that density alone will add "more inherently affordable housing types and tenures (i.e. smaller units, rental units).   Then it claims that density helps increase supply which then moderates price increases, helps make car ownership less necessary and promotes secondary suites and coach houses.

An article by Pieta Wooley in the November 29, 2007 issue of *The Georgia Straight* provides some data to negate the argument that increased density *per se* helps moderate housing prices. It is pointed out that for the fifteen years between 1991 and 2006, Vancouver grew by about 106,000 people and added about 69,000 housing units. At a rate of 2.2 people per unit, that would translate into accommodations for 151,800 people, almost 50% more than needed.   By this data, housing prices should have been stable, even lower.   But in fact housing prices *doubled* over that period.   In 2007, 3,294 new condo units were completed in downtown alone, most of these units reaching unheard of prices of some $800 per square foot.

Accordingly, the data disproves the central theory of EcoDensity, insofar as it purports to tackle housing affordability through density alone.

By June 10, 2008, the revised draft of EcoDensity was approved. The first draft was tweaked a little to provide more options for rental secondary suites and back-yard and laneway housing.   Of course those are options that help existing homeowners "mine" greater profits from their existing properties.   Moreover those matters were delayed for implementation until 2009.   The parts of EcoDensity that were to take effect immediately were rezoning policies for greener buildings and greener larger sites.   Again, Vancouver managed, in the guise of EcoDensity, to create greater value for existing homeowners and greater costs for new condo owners as their developments will have all sorts of new costs imposed on them.   These include meeting green standards of the LEED (Leadership in Energy and Environmental Design) Program and, for large sites, the development of district energy systems (supplying heat or electricity to the area) and even what is called a "sustainable transportation demand-management strategy" (figuring out how to reduce vehicle traffic in and out of the area).

Accordingly, the winners again are developer/builders large enough to tackle the increased complexity and costs (cutting out smaller builders who might build less expensive projects) and the boomer residents who will now be able to develop their laneway garages into small suites for more rental income or to house their children who have no hope otherwise of affording homes here. The losers are those young people and new immigrants who will be forced to pay all the environmental costs of the new developments.

Vision Councilor Raymond Louie spoke out for the provision of defined goals for affordability in new major projects, rather than leaving it up to planners to do the traditional bargaining with developers on a case by case basis. The NPA's Peter Ladner was opposed to objective affordability targets. No one cited the plethora of affordable housing programs in the Rest of Canada or the U.S., as we shall outline later in this chapter. Instead, as Frances Bula wrote in the June 12, 2008 edition of the *Vancouver Sun,* "EcoDensity is now a name and a plan that is admired in other cities." Once again, it is all about recognition, branding and appearances; the actual effect on the possibilities for young people to raise families in affordable homes in Vancouver seems less important.

One of the main reasons for the continuous increase in prices of new condos in the early 2000s, was that the apparent discrepancy between supply and demand in fact resulted from many of the condos being purchased by "investors". To understand the issue, we can turn to the guru of condo marketing in Vancouver, Bob Rennie. At a speech to the Urban Development Institute in May, 2007, Rennie made the following points:

1. Every time we acknowledge that investors are buying 30%, 40% or 50% of a new tower, there is an outcry "It is a bubble. It can't last. These are not real buyers."

Remember, says Rennie, without the investor, we would have a rental crisis. Worse than the pressure that is about to come.

2. Investors have 15 – 25% deposits.

3. Our statistics show that only 25% of those investors resell or assign prior to completion. A very interesting fact – investors typically do not buy finished product.
It is simple. They want leverage. For them it's not about the cap rate/rental return.
It's all about equity gain. Investors – once they see the capital appreciation, they are happy and will hold.

And so, Rennie makes clear the extent to which the condo boom in Vancouver is a poor substitute for a proper market of new rental units; at the same time, he makes clear that the system is predicated on capital gains to investors, and hence increasing prices for the end-users. The big winners, aside from Rennie, himself, then, are the developers and the investors. This is perfectly acceptable to existing residents of Vancouver because the value of *their* housing goes up in tandem with the new housing, gradually enriching them just as surely as it impoverishes the end-users of the new housing being built. It is a corrupt and socially unjust housing system, and it is an essential component of the greed inherent in Vancouverism.

If in fact the American recession in housing prices does spread to Vancouver, then perhaps some of the investors or speculators holding condo units may not be able to sell them or rent them for high rents. This could result in these units being rented for whatever the market might allow, and thus a recession might be some help for those seeking more affordable rentals (as long as they still have jobs!).

In the realm of social housing, the City by late December, 2007 did approve a twelve-site social housing project to create supportive and social housing on existing city-owned properties, in partnership with the provincial housing authority. The City of course is to be praised for making this effort, belated or not, to reduce homelessness and house the mentally ill in supportive housing. It is interesting that it took the fact of the Olympic Games, and how we would look to the "outside world" to prompt us to do what should have been done before. Mayor Sam Sullivan made this clear, in a *Vancouver Sun,* article on December 21st: "I have told the federal and provincial governments that Vancouver is going to represent the country (in 2010) and I don't think you want the world to see what we've got right now." As usual, it is how we look to others that matters, not what is intrinsically the right thing to do. But better to do the right thing for the wrong reasons than not to do it at all.

In addition, Vancouverites will often fight against any social housing proposed for their neighbourhoods. This is called "NIMBY-ism" – "Not In My Backyard". In Lotus Land, however, people go farther – there is a group called NIABY – "Not In Anybody's Back Yard" which opposes the location of drug treatment centres and other facilities for the mentally ill *anywhere.* This shows that even when the municipal politicians are prepared to lead, when it comes to desperately needed facilities, the ideology of Lotus Land is uncaring and in fact oppositional to anything that might affect the cherished goal of high property values.

So with the exception of this program for the 12 sites, announced in December, 2007, is there really any evidence of a commitment to affordable housing as a key value? Or is it more of a case of making the assumption that more density, like in Downtown, as it spreads to other areas, will conduce somehow to affordability. And is it more of a case that density can be accepted if the prices are high enough to limit the tenants to the "right kind" of people?

Obligating new development to be "greener" is of course well in keeping with the usual environmentalism of the Lotos-Eaters: let others pay for environmental sustainability; we support environmentalism, as long as we do not have to pay for it. Let the new residents pay for Eco-Density, just don't raise our taxes, or compel the existing residents to upgrade our properties to reduce *our* ecological footprints.

While you are at it, make the developers pay for amenities like parks and libraries, which will then be added to the cost of the housing, so that existing residents will not have to pay for additional amenities through their property taxes. Instead, forcing up the price of new housing automatically increases the property values of existing homes, which is a nice deal for the baby-boomers who "got in early".

We know that density Downtown has not assisted affordability, and has not provided the range of housing to meet the diverse needs of our population. Why should we assume that the program of EcoDensity will be any different?

The answer is that EcoDensity, so far, is just a sound bite. It sounds good, sounds as if we are using the most up-to-date policies to create a dense urbanism which still respects the environment. We hope that a groundswell of criticism will arise to push Vancouver's recalcitrant politicians and planners into something better – shall we call it *Eco-afforda-density*?

To the many condo owners now facing large special assessments to repair their leaky condos, the idea that Vancouver is a leader in Green construction or a leader in any type of construction is a cruel joke. The fact is that before we make policy on the basis of building sustainability, we might question how sustainable are the poorly built condos, designed by some of our big name architects (for example, Arthur Erickson was the architect for some horrible leaky condo buildings) and built by developers still doing a large business here, but legally untouchable because they use separate corporations for each project. There are many interesting problems with condos in Vancouver. How can a bank take a mortgage with an amortization of 30, even 40 years on a building which probably has a lifespan of 15?

Not only is "sustainability" something of a joke to the hapless owners of leaky condos, the concept of "livability", so often stressed by those promoting EcoDensity, is also a cruel joke. When the failure of the building envelope has created leaks and resultant toxic mold many people found their condos to be *un*livable.

Here, according to the website www.bcdex.com of the British Columbia Construction and Landscaping Network, are the sad figures for all of British Columbia for the leaky condo tragedy:

- Registered leaky condos across B.C.: 900 buildings, 31,037 individual units,
- Estimate of the total number of affected units: 50,000,
- Average cost of repairs per condo unit: $21,040,
- Average cost of repairs per co-op unit: $34,000,
- Estimate of the total cost of repairs: $1 Billion,
- Estimated indirect costs of the leaky condo crisis: $2 Billion,

There were some modest programs in response, such as interest free loans for repairs, provincial waiver of sales tax on repairs, and the institution of a new warranty program warranting the building envelope against water penetration for five years; however, the municipalities, the province and the federal government's Canada Mortgage and Housing Corporation were able for the most part, to avoid substantial payouts   - leaving no adequate governmental response for those who lost out so horribly in the real estate game that made so many others wealthy.   One can assume that there will arise cases of water penetration *after* five years, so the problem will continue.

In part, the problem has been "covered up" by the inflation of housing prices between 2002 and 2007;   that is, in some cases the cost of repairs have been exceeded by the increased value of the unit.   But in many cases, the strata boards have done inadequate repairs, sufficient only to allow the current owners to get out with a small profit.   When prices stabilize, or even decrease, the leaky condo problem will again rear its head, in those buildings that have yet to show problems within the 5 year warranty term or have shown problems, which have been inadequately remediated.

One reluctantly draws the conclusion that the words, "sustainability", "livability" and "affordability", when used by Vancouver politicians, are quite meaningless.   One gets the impression that both the media, which relies on developer's advertising, and the municipal politicians, who receive political donations from developers, in reality act as shills for the elaborate marketing game that is the marketing of Vancouver condos.

However, the reader might ask, since the construction of more high rise condo units does not seem to bring more affordable prices, what could the City do to promote *affordable housing?* Let us discuss briefly a ten-point plan that might actually be effective to address the problem, assuming people want to address the problem.

There are two main delivery models for affordable rental or owned housing for low to moderate income working people. One depends on the establishment of Community Housing Trusts, as discussed in Chapter 4, which create what we call "off-market" housing that stays affordable due to restrictive covenants on the title. The other is rental housing provided by the private sector - but made financially feasible by various financial inducements provided by government, in return for long-term operating agreements stipulating permitted rents and income levels, adherence to which results in forgiveness of government loans.

Municipalities can establish their own Community Housing Trusts (sometimes called Community Land Trusts), and finance them in a variety of ways, some of which are listed below. Alternatively, they can establish what are usually called Affordable Housing Funds, which can fund Community Housing Trusts, or act as a source of municipal inducements to private sector affordable housing developers.

Whichever vehicle is used, here are some ways to create municipally generated affordable housing, and some ways to induce private sector participation. Because municipalities are only allowed the powers given to them by provincial law, some of these techniques would have to be authorized by provincial law reform:

1. Obligate large developers as a condition of development approval of large projects to pay a certain sum into the Community Housing Trust or Affordable Housing Fund for each unit, or transfer title to a certain number of units directly to a Community Housing Trust. This would replace the present practice of developers being required to spend money on certain public amenities and return the cost of public amenities to the wider tax base.

2. If our planning process is being used by large developers to create investment units for high income individuals from out of the province, who are not even bothering to rent them out, we should follow Gregor Robertson's policy proposal of taxing them at a business property tax rate and/or creating a special tax on sale. It is time that we realized that our precious housing stock should be used for the benefit of our residents, not as speculative investment vehicles for non-residents.

3. Create certain dedicated sources of funding for the Community Housing Trust or the Affordable Housing Fund.

    (a) For example, the city of Victoria pays all of its G.S.T. rebate fund of approximately $200,000 per year into its Community Land Trust.

    (b) Given that Vancouver property taxes are often about 60% of property taxes on similarly valued properties in other cities, there is room to place an "affordable housing surcharge" on tax bills, with the requirement that this surcharge only be used for affordable housing in one of the two models being discussed.

    (c) There should be a "demolition tax" of approximately $20,000 for every unit being demolished to make way for fancier new housing. The process of densification in the real world of Vancouver development often means that a modest starter bungalow is demolished in favour of two or three high end duplex or triplex units. If the developer had to pay $20,000 when developing units which often sell for $1 million, or more, the extra cost would not be prohibitive, but would help make up for the fact that the city has lost the demolished modest housing. At present, the demolition permit fee is only $1000. per unit demolished.

(d) The Province should be strongly lobbied to return a certain percentage of the massive amount of Property Transfer Taxes and that should be paid into the Community Housing Trust or Affordable Housing Fund.

(e) Right now business pays about six times as much property tax as residences of the same value. All this does is subsidize wealthy individual property owners at the cost of economic competitiveness to business. It would be much wiser to reduce the property taxes of large businesses in return for them assisting in the provision of "workforce housing", by providing either land or money to the Community Housing Trust or Affordable Housing Fund.

4. The municipality can provide grants equal to development cost charges and building permit fees for affordable housing projects.

5. As is done in the State of Florida, affordable housing projects can move to the head of the line, with so-called "expedited processing".

6. In cases where the units will be priced affordably, the City, if authorized by the Province, can institute a brownfield remediation tax assistance program. This means that any costs to clean up environmental

contamination on the site, can be offset against property taxes for the new development.

7. Density bonuses can be granted for a specified number of affordably priced units, preferably to be conveyed to the Community Housing Trust, to keep them affordable forever.

8. The School Board should be encouraged, in cases of schools with declining enrolments and surplus land, to convey the land to the Community Housing Trust for the construction of family housing, which will restore the targeted enrolment. The school would lose some of its large playground, but parents would be happy to save the neighbourhood school.

9. For every neighbourhood, there should be a comparison of the amount of parkland per capita and the amount of affordable housing per capita, and if the ratio of parkland to affordable housing is too high, then some of the parkland should be conveyed to the Community Housing Trust. The other option would be to sell part of the excessive parkland for other residential development with the proceeds of sale to go to the Community Housing Trust or Affordable Housing Fund. There should be a consideration of adding additional units above existing parkland caretakers' cottages and washrooms, which could be used to house lower income municipal workers if desired.

10. When creating new rapid transit stations, the City should be allowed to use its expropriation power to expropriate all the property around the new station at the pre-station values. Then it could use the land adjacent to these stations for the development of affordable housing in a location where automobiles would not be necessary. This would be preferable to simply enriching the adjoining landowners who will sell out anyway to developers of higher priced housing.

11. Municipal surplus sites should be conveyed to the Community Housing Trust, or, if not suitable for housing, should be sold with the proceeds going into

the Community Housing Trust or Affordable Housing Fund.

Accordingly, one can see that there are a plethora of ways that a municipality can promote affordable housing. The Community Housing Trust model is extremely suitable for a place like Vancouver, where lack of new developable land is creating a wild inflation of land values. The Community Housing Trust model allows for the setting aside of a certain percentage of housing for moderate income working people, without whom no city can function. The buyers of units in the Community Housing Trust get their units at a discount to market value as a result of the cost savings resulting from the utilization of the methods discussed above. The buyer, in return for a lower price on his/her unit and a lower carrying cost, gives up much of the capital gain on resale, so that the unit remains affordable to the next buyer.

There are, then, established ways of proceeding, even in the absence of federal-provincial programs. The municipality can do much. If we choose not to pursue affordable housing because of greed and not caring, then I believe that we are indeed creating a fraud on the young.

As discussed in Chapter 2, there are programs in effect that are benefiting seniors *without a means test*. Mostly, these are provincial programs. They should be altered immediately so that only *needy* seniors will get the benefits. We have a crisis in terms of housing those young people who are not fortunate enough to have wealthy parents. They deserve our help. The stability of society in the coming years requires our help. If we do not give such help, then we are no better than Tennyson's mariners - who abandoned their young because they were concerned only with their own enjoyment of the Lotos.

I agree that Global Warming is a problem. But the way that the Lotos-Eaters have made it the only problem worthy of their concern is highly suspect. It is suspect, but understandable, given the ideology of the Lotos.   Other ideologies might be concerned about other things too. For example:

1. While some experts on climate change project thousands of deaths in Africa from heat and drought related causes, there are thousands of deaths occurring *right now* from genocide in Darfur, and thousands of deaths of young Muslims by internecine strife between Shia and Sunni, and between fundamentalists and secularists, together with terrorism.

2. While we prioritize green building design, density, and land use, we overlook hundreds of deaths now of young drivers, drunk drivers, and those who could have been out of their cars, if we prioritized rapid transit into the suburbs. Moreover, am I the only one that thinks that reduced automobile use due to a good system of public transit, is a far greater environmental dictate than LEED designed high-rises? To be sure, we do not want low density urban sprawl, but that issue could be better dealt with if Vancouver would see itself more properly as just one component of Metro Vancouver, be less self-absorbed about how to fit more and more people into less and less land, and work with the suburbs on good, dense, and walkable nodes of development in the suburbs, linked to each other and Vancouver by rapid transit.   Let us see how willing Vancouver is in the future to pay a fair share of the proposed rapid transit in the suburbs, or whether, as usual, the owners of the million dollar homes in Vancouver will be looking for someone else to pay the bills.

3. While we prioritize green building design, we are losing young people to the ravages of drugs and HIV/AIDS in the Downtown Eastside and elsewhere. Higher spending on those problems, while not as "sexy" as green building design and roof-top gardens, would do more to save lives now.

4. As noted in Chapter 7, we are witnessing the death of young people, including innocent bystanders, through a

confused drug policy and inadequate policing and justice system, with regard to gangs.

As Vancouver promotes its EcoDensity program, is there any real research on what steps planners can take to give the best financial return on dollars spent in the area of global warming and climate change? Or are we just leaping into a program that just happens to perpetuate the Vancouver Model of high density, high cost, condos that inadequately serve our diverse population? Might our politicians be too cozy with the large developers in whose interest it is to promote this model?

Actually the problem is far wider than that. The wider population in Vancouver mostly misunderstands the importance of inducing the creation of more rental units – at all levels of affordability. For if there are no new rental units being constructed, then the rental market, one way or another, legally or illegally, will become more and more expensive.

The best example that I can give of this misunderstanding is the coverage by *The Vancouver Courier* on June 27, 2008 of news of the plans by the Siddoo family (owners of several large rental buildings) to convert their recently purchased Coast Plaza Hotel back to rental apartments. This building is in Downtown's West End, Vancouver's prime area for renting smaller units, where 82% of residents are renters (totaling 25,285 rental households). The article points out that the vacancy rate in the West End has been at a record low for the last three years. We know that when the vacancy rate becomes so low, landlords can obtain illegal rent increases just by threatening to do renovations and raise the rent. B.C. does not have the legal protection for tenants that Ontario has, where there is a law that if the landlord must do renovations or repairs, the tenant has a first right of refusal to take the unit again when the repairs are finished. In B.C. renovations are often just a sham to provide for increased rents far in excess of what the renovations would justify.

So in the absence of legal protections, inducing the private sector into creating more rental units should be the first priority. But the *Courier* article, which should have been completely celebratory, had a by-line stating that "Proposal raises questions about unit affordability". In the article, Brant Granby, president of the West End Residents Association is quoted on his concern whether the building will be affordable or not. At the same time, Granby points out the list of amenities he would like to see the developer create – such things as daycare or program rooms for a support centre for gay, lesbians and transgendered people.

The transformation of the hotel to a rental apartment building requires a rezoning. Therefore the residents' demands for amenities will be raised and the developer will likely have to spend the extra money on consultants' meetings with the residents, hearings, perhaps appeals, and then the cost of the amenities. Does no-one understand that the costs of the amenities should be shared by all property tax payers? Does no-one understand that the creation of rental units is so necessary that this is a one-hundred percent good news story, no matter what the rents will be? That is because the creation of 316 rental apartments (as opposed to a hotel) will help the vacancy rates and that will help *all* tenants. And the shopping list of developer-provided amenities will help to guarantee higher rents. Not a lot of developers are willing to do what the Siddoos are doing. They should be encouraged, but the very people who will benefit most are throwing up roadblocks, adding additional costs, and failing to understand the very nature of who is responsible for creating neighbourhood amenities, and that in the private sector, costs have to be passed on, if a developer is going to be induced to do something that also happens to be in the public interest. Instead we shackle developers with more and more costs, and now we are going to impose the environmental upgrades of the Eco-Density program. It is time for Vancouverites to comprehend just who it is who actually pays for these programs.

There are all kinds of structural reasons that drive up Vancouver housing costs, and then pervert the end result. I am thinking in particular of the policy that the cost of major planning studies for major rezoning projects is paid by the developer-proponent. For example, *The Vancouver Courier,* in an August 1, 2008 article by Cheryl Rossi, pointed out that the owner of the Arbutus Centre shopping mall paid the city the $397,000 cost of policy planning with respect to its proposal to add up to 650 condo units to its commercial property.

Georgina Spilos, the chair of a residents' group opposing the plan says her group is so opposed to the process that it has filed a complaint against the City with the provincial Ombudsman's office: "We want them to look at the impact of this cost-recovery process on the entire planning program. If the developer pays the bill, does it affect the final result."

In the *Courier* story, Dwayne Drobot, a city planner with the major projects group, said that the practice of developers paying for a policy plan for its site has been standard since the early '90s, and the purpose, he said, was so that *developers, not taxpayers*, pay the cost. But, as we have seen elsewhere in this book, costs that are directed away from all the taxpayers, and are imposed on the developer just end up being passed along to the homebuyers, in the way of higher home prices. Not only does the process give the appearance to neighbours that the city is "in bed" with the developer who is paying for the cost of the planning studies, but the process ends up costing future residents money and thus pushes up all Vancouver housing prices. Of course, that is fine with the existing residents, whose taxes are kept low because the cost of the studies was funded indirectly, by future residents, and the process ends up pushing up the value of *their existing* homes. It is only a problem if you are concerned about your children and other new residents having somewhere affordable to live.

Moreover, shouldn't we be a little suspect of politicians talking EcoDensity, while we have substandard sewage treatment plants and we have to soon take all of our garbage to Washington State, because we are not inclined to dump it anywhere in our own City, Region, or even Country, and residents are invariably opposed to the location of waste-to-energy incineration plants anywhere near their neighbourhoods?

And let us return again to the problem of the homeless. While we spend our time on EcoDensity and neglect inducements for the construction of affordable rental housing and neglect better policies for the drug addicted and mentally ill, we have larger and larger numbers of people sleeping in parks. According to Parks Board Commissioner Spencer Hubert, interviewed in *The Vancouver Courier* on August 6, 2008, there are an estimated 1600 people living on the streets of Vancouver. There are only 700 shelter beds. Accordingly a large number of people sleep in city parks, including Stanley Park and the Downtown Eastside's Openheimer Park.

One problem (besides the obvious one of why the other residents of "The Best Place on Earth" feel that this is acceptable) is that a City by-law prohibits camping in parks overnight. So the poor police, charged with administering the by-law often let the homeless sleep until 3:00 or 4:00 a.m. and then wake them up and move them on. Not allowing people, some of whom are mentally ill to begin with, to have a full night of sleep, is cruel, to say the least.

Herbert, whose heart is in the right place, says that while parks should not be transformed into campgrounds, some provision must be made for the homeless, and he suggests that it may be time to consider a tent city for the homeless, with washrooms and social workers.

Again, we have a situation where the Lotus Land anti-Americans are missing out on good ideas due to the reluctance to admit that many American cities are more progressive that Vancouver, and the supposed "Best Place on Earth" has something to learn.

In the *Courier* article, reporter Sandra Thomas makes the point that Seattle has two tent cities organized by the Seattle Housing and Resource Efforts (SHARE), and the Women's Housing, Equality and Enhancement League. What I think is brilliant about these tent cities (created eight years ago now!) is that they move to a different location every 90 days, to minimize permanent negative impact on host neighbourhoods.

I leave it to Mr. Herbert to conclude: "We need to mature as a society. Cracking down (by police) is only a short-term fix. This needs more mature solutions." Bravo.

Let's realize that many young visitors to Vancouver, who later settled down here into middle class life, at one time or another might have slept on a beach like a Lotos Eater.

Elementary social justice requires us to take care of the unfortunates who cannot seem to move beyond sleeping in parks and beaches. Let's get rid of slogans like EcoDensity and truly aspire to be a "Best Place on Earth".

But for now, when the Lotos-Eaters are mostly interested in the calm and beauty of Lotus Land, then I believe that vague statements about the environment, and the implementation of policies that will cost somebody else money, mean that they should be seen for the uncaring rich and self-satisfied Lotos-Eaters that they are.   I suggest that all of this is an outright fraud on our young.

Chapter 10

White Collar Crime in the Wild West

"Let what is broken so remain.
The Gods are hard to reconcile:
'Tis hard to settle order once again.
There is confusion worse than death,
Trouble on trouble, pain on pain,
Long labour unto aged breath,
Sore task to hearts worn out by many wars
And eyes grown dim with gazing on the pilot-stars …

… Let us swear an oath, and keep it with an equal mind,
In the hollow Lotos-land to live and lie reclined
On the hills like Gods together, careless of mankind"

Alfred Tennyson, "The Lotos-Eaters"

"You can choose a ready guide in some celestial voice
If you choose not to decide, you still have made a choice
You can choose from phantom fears and kindness that can kill
I will choose a path that's clear
I will choose freewill"

Neil Peart and Rush, "Freewill", from the album *Permanent Waves*,
1980

It must be the worst kept secret in Canada: Vancouver is full of
scammers, fraud artists, unethical stock promoters, "investor relations"
mouthpieces, internet fraudsters, and every other type of white collar
criminal that greed and lack of ethics has ever invented.

Is there something inherent in the ethos of Lotus Land that creates and nurtures, and then refuses to properly sanction and punish, white collar criminals?

Isn't it quite simple? In the land of the Lotos, where harvesting the Lotos fruit is available without a "life of toil", and where moral questions of Good and Evil have been banished, fast and easy money is the ethos; "crime" is only applicable to those who either "get caught" or misunderstand the precise location of the line between criminal and non-criminal behaviour, between cleverness and fraud.

In Lotus Land, therefore, even those who are found guilty of white collar crime, receive only a slap on the wrist. When fraud, dishonesty and corruption are so endemic, why come down too hard on the poor guys who simply lack sophistication in their dishonest ways?

Moreover, in Lotus Land, crime is increasingly regarded as a normal aspect of the social and economic system, rather than as disruption or deviance. White collar crime, then, is a *normal aspect* of the *economic system*, based on Vancouver's history of investment fraud and other white collar crime.

In the narcissistic world of Lotus Land, we have somehow accepted the moral monstrosity that white collar crime hurts the criminal more than anyone else. How many judges emphasize the disgrace and loss of reputation as they give a minor, knuckle-rapping penalty to the white collar criminal? What about the damage done to the victims? What about the importance of *denouncing* this behaviour? A good example of the state of mind of the narcissistic white collar criminal were the words of Conrad Black's associate, and Vancouver resident David Radler, at his sentencing hearing for taking part in a $30 million fraud scheme: "I made mistakes, I hurt myself, my family and others. I am sorry for the suffering to my family and others,"

So his first words were that he hurt himself. Then he acknowledges that he hurt his family, then "others". The white-collar criminal in

Lotus Land doesn't think too much about the "others" who he has hurt, being so totally focused on himself.

British criminologist John Lea is one of the current members of the "Left Realist" school of criminology. In a 2001 paper, given at the annual conference of the German Criminological Association, he stated:

"The fact that crime becomes a normalized risk of postmodern life and the identity of criminal offenders becomes blurred, implies also, as its accompaniment, the normalization of activities and motivations hitherto considered criminal. Crime becomes an increasingly normal activity to be entered into... Criminals are no longer ...seeking status by deviant means, they are just doing what everyone else is doing. Crime is increasingly '...generated less by a deficit than a hypertrophy of opportunities... the effect of the gigantic and uncontrolled proliferation of ways in which status can be achieved...' (quoting Italian criminologist Vincenzo Ruggiero).

"All these themes relate to a perceived process of social and economic fragmentation characteristic of 'postmodern'... with an implied weakening of the distinctions between normal and pathological, culture and subculture, moral and immoral."

Let us look at how the history of white collar crime in Vancouver has weakened the "distinctions between normal and pathological, culture and subculture, moral and immoral."

The 1987 book, *Fleecing the Lamb: The Inside Story of the Vancouver Stock Exchange*, by Cruise and Griffiths, tells a very complete story of the old Vancouver Stock Exchange. The VSE, together with the Alberta Stock Exchange, merged into what is now known as the TSX – Venture Exchange. That was after the scandals of Bre-X and Cartaway Resources, although both were Alberta Stock Exchange listings. The history of corruption in the trading of junior equities in the VSE, however, brought it to a close with the 1999 merger.

The book tells the story of how the Toronto Stock Exchange turned its back on the junior stock promoters after the scandal pertaining to Windfall Resources. This was the impetus for the junior stocks, and their promoters, such as Murray Pezim, to come west. Initially, Pezim made his name with successes like the Hemlo Gold Fields, then progressed to become the best known "promoter" in Vancouver, until he was suspended for 1 year for insider trading, and gradually faded from the scene.

The basic fault with the VSE junior companies was that most seemed to be much more interested in promoting the stock value, than building the underlying businesses. In the Wild West atmosphere of an inadequately regulated stock exchange, questionable "promoters" would, sometimes with the participation of brokers and lawyers, take shares in a company, which was promoted as about to acquire some property, or have a property that was going to yield great returns, so that the stock would go up wildly, and the promoters and their friends would sell out, before the stock crashed back to earth, since there really was no good underlying business. The odd thing is that most people knew the promoters were less than honest, yet people still wanted in on the greedy game. Just look at some of the nicknames used for the promoters and financiers. According to *Vancouver Sun* business reporter David Baines, in a lecture to the Vancouver Historical Society in November, 2007, (entitled "Lambs to the Slaughter: How and why Vancouver became a haven for penny stock crooks") Gus McPhail became known as the "thief", Murray Pezim as the "butcher" and Peter Brown as the "undertaker".

During the mid-1980s Edward Carter and David Ward manipulated, through 100 trading accounts distributed among 15 brokerage firms in Canada, the U.S. and the Cayman Islands, the shares of 19 worthless public companies listed on the Vancouver Stock Exchange. In addition, Carter and Ward paid secret commissions to the portfolio manager of an American-based mutual fund in return for his purchase of large volumes of stock in the target companies. Oddly enough, when these actions came to light the regulators allowed the promoters to buy the stock back from the mutual fund. An "old boys network" was in effect, instead of a vigorous Securities Commission to protect the interests of the public.

By 1989, *Forbes* magazine did an article calling Vancouver the "Scam Capital of the World".

In the later 1990s, a number of Vancouver brokerage firms and their executives were disciplined for insider trading, improper supervision, conflict of interest, and conduct contrary to the public interest.

Vancouver's Yorkton Securities used to attract much criticism and scrutiny for issuing "strong buy" recommendations on tech stocks that some of its analysts had heavily invested in before they went public.

Executives such a G. Scott Paterson and Pier Donnini in the Book4Golf and Xencet fiascos received large fines and suspensions from trading.

According to Advisor.ca, Yorkton and Paterson did not disclose to clients that some of the technology stocks they promoted were of companies owned in part by Yorkton and its executives. In some cases, executives also helped found the firms, were the directors of the companies, sat on their boards or were the underwriters and financiers.

Between 1997 and 2000, Paterson wore many hats as director and shareholder of some of the companies, while also an executive at Yorkton. Paterson, and fellow executives Roger Dent, Nelson Smith and Alkarim Jirvaj purchased shares of companies while they assisted with their financing and were aware of undisclosed information. Dent, director of research at Yorkton, didn't ensure that research reports identified his position as a director of one of the tech companies — a conflict of interest.

Vancouver's public markets attracted an undue number of "pump and dump" scammers, traders through anonymous offshore accounts, and promoters of companies with no viable business prospects where the main business was stock promotion and manipulation - to the benefit of the promoters and early stage executives and to the detriment of investors.

In some cases, like that of Turbodyne Technologies Inc., a VSE listed company, fraudulent business announcements operated in tandem with monies paid to questionable firms promoting the shares to European investors.

After large numbers of abuses, and a failure of due regulation, the Vancouver Stock Exchange and the Alberta Stock Exchange in 1999 merged into something called the Canadian Venture Exchange, which was meant to specialize in junior stocks seeking capital for mineral exploration or new technology ventures.

By 2001, that was acquired by the TSX Group and renamed the TSX Venture Exchange.

But the Vancouver fraudsters and scammers moved on to a less regulated environment where they could continue their white collar crime – the OTC Bulletin Board in the United States, where, according to the *Sun's* David Baines, some 500 to 800 Vancouver based companies were listed by 2006 and were "now spreading over the land like locusts".

Another playground for Vancouver fraudsters is the so-called "Pink Sheets", which is in fact not a regulated stock exchange at all, where a company must apply to be listed, but an unregulated computer to computer trading system used by certain brokers.

But even the companies on the OTC (over the counter) Bulletin Board are suspect, as there are inadequate disclosure regulations and rampant insider trading.   The target market is naïve American investors, and the promoters continue the old scam of having insiders with offshore accounts trade shares back and forth with each other to bid up the price of shares, as they gradually dump them off to investors who soon take the hit from shares with no underlying business value.

Finally, on December 3, 2007, the B.C. Securities Commission released proposed rules, which, if adopted, should address the huge number of rigged public companies with sham businesses emanating out of Vancouver. Until now, promoters were able to bypass B.C. regulations by selling shares under exemptions to family and close friends, to be traded on the Pink Sheets or OTC Bulletin Board. They then gathered back all the shares, the price of which were able to be easily manipulated, with "fake" shareholders and sham business ventures. According to *The Vancouver Sun's* David Baines, 70% of all Canadian based companies trading on the U.S. over the counter markets were B.C. based.

Now, hopefully, regulations will be enacted making it illegal for the "seed" shareholders in B.C. to sell their stock back to promoters. Rather they will have to sell their shares through brokers from accounts in their own names, making such actions public and viewable by other potential investors. Moreover, brokers will be required to know who beneficially owns an OTC stock before it is traded, and will not be able to accept delivery of the OTC stock until a provincial compliance officer approves same. This is intended to curb the use of local brokerages by share manipulators and money-launderers.

Given the number of fraudsters and scammers among us in Vancouver, one can be forgiven for some skepticism - the stock fraudsters will probably find a new vehicle for their frauds. Already Vancouver has numerous internet scam artists, some illegally reselling Canadian lottery tickets abroad, or committing outright fraud by promising lottery winnings in return for "administrative" fees. Other Vancouverites are involved with internet-based identity theft and credit card fraud. Still others are importing "counterfeit" brand merchandise. As Sgt. Dany Bernier of the RCMP's Border Integrity Federal Enforcement Section has said (quoted in the June 17, 2008 *Vancouver Sun*): Vancouver "is one of the largest gateways for counterfeit products to North America."

And these counterfeit products are not just limited to fake Gucci handbags and Nike branded sports equipment. More dangerous are the counterfeit drugs entering North America through Vancouver. These drugs (a high percentage of which are counterfeit erectile dysfunction medications sold over the internet) often contain either too much or too little of the active ingredients, or may contain other chemicals that are untested. Accordingly, these counterfeit drugs may be costing lives.

What remains to be seen is whether B.C. courts will start to give serious sentences to white collar criminals. If not, then Greater Vancouver will retain its standing as a hospitable locality for fraudsters. David Baines on November 9, 2007 reported on the case of Gordon Garritty of White Rock, just outside Vancouver, who pleaded guilty to defrauding an insurance company by issuing about 100 fraudulent leaky condo repair insurance policies. These were policies meant to protect condominium complexes who were retaining contractors to repair leaky condos, as repair contractors were required by a provincial law to carry insurance. Garritty, between January 2001 and May 2004, sold policies that he falsely claimed were underwritten by Kingsway General Insurance Co. He filed documents with the Homeowners Protection office certifying that insurance was issued, when in fact it had not been. He received some $2 million in premiums that exposed Kingsway to potential liability of $26 million.

Almost 2 years after selling the first policy, Garritty began to account to Kingsway for premiums collected, but then fraudulently reported the premiums as collected on new home construction. In addition, he improperly retained half of the premiums for commission and administrative expenses, and did not reflect this on paperwork sent to Kingsway.

Both the Crown prosecutor and defense counsel agreed that a conditional sentence of two years less a day would be appropriate. The Judge, however, decided that an 18 month sentence, to be served in the community, was sufficient.

Once again, we see that Lotus Land is incapable of denouncing the conduct of white collar criminals. Whether B.C. is the "best place on earth" may be debatable, but it is clearly the best place on earth to be a white collar criminal.

The one offense to stay away from, however, in Vancouver, is illegally cutting trees on your property. In Lotus Land, it seems to be the most heinous of all crimes. In 2006, a West side lady was fined $14,000 or $500 per tree for illegally cutting down 28 Douglas firs and Western Red Cedars at the back of her 100 foot by 400 foot Point Grey property. The minimum fine for each tree cut down is $500 and the maximum is $20,000.

In 2007, a local realtor was fined $205,000, or $2,850 per tree, for the removal in 2005 of 72 trees on three Belmont Avenue properties in Point Grey.

And in 1997, Vancouver socialite and philanthropist Jacqueline Cohen paid more than $50,000 to the GVRD and apologized after someone cut down 35 50-year-old oaks in Pacific Spirit Park in front of her home in the 5800-block of Northwest Marine Drive.

In an article by Naoibh O'Connor in *The Vancouver Courier* on January 16, 2008 city official Rick Michaels explained the rationale of the law: "The tree bylaw, if you go back to its origins, there are two elements. One is protecting the urban forest of Vancouver, but there's also this important aspect of looking after the environment and this is one important measure towards doing that," he said.

According to the *Courier* article: "Property owners must get approval from city hall to chop down any tree with a trunk diameter of eight inches or more, measured 1.2 metres from the ground, according to the city's private property tree bylaw. A person can remove one tree a year with a permit, although authorization is often contingent on planting a replacement tree. Any subsequent trees removed must be accompanied by an arborist report indicating the tree is dying or is a hazard. Other trees can be removed with city permits if they're on land where a new house or garage will be built."

Then, a 72 year old well-known interior designer whose beach front expensive condo had its view of the ocean blocked by some trees, came up with a novel idea to get rid of the trees without cutting them: she *poisoned* the trees. Some of the trees then died, but rather than charging her with a breach of the tree protection by-law, the diligent law enforcers charged her with public mischief, opening the way for fines and/or a jail sentence.

Fortunately for her, the Judge, after she voluntarily paid $50,000 to plant new trees, decided that she had suffered enough and gave her a discharge. And suffered she had, at the hands of angry Vancouver environmentalists. These environmental vigilantes, finding out where she lived, pelted her condo with dog feces and garbage, eventually forcing the woman to sell her prized condo, and give up her interior design business. Her lawyer, talking to CBCNews.ca, called what happened to her a "complete incineration of a lifetime of achievement" and said what she did was an "amateur act of an elderly woman who got an idea in her head." There is not too much that gets the Lotos Eaters worked up, but this poor lady found out that, when it comes to trees, you cannot mess with the Lotos Eaters.

It is a lot harder to get rid of a tree in Vancouver than it is to steal money from an investor – and the penalties and public disgrace for illegally cutting down the tree seem to be much harsher than for stock fraud. To me, that is a appropriate symbol for the ethos of Lotus Land.

Chapter 11

The Starbucks "Progressives" and the Ascent of "Tolerism"

"In the afternoon they came unto a land
In which it seemed always afternoon."

From "The Lotos Eaters", Alfred Tennyson

"The cook took the cauldron of soup off the fire, and at once set to work throwing every thing within her reach at the Duchess and the baby — the fire-irons came first; then followed a shower of saucepans, plates, and dishes. . . 'If everyone minded their own business', the Duchess said, in a hoarse growl, 'the world would go round a deal faster than it does'. . . 'which would not be an advantage', said Alice, who felt very glad to get an opportunity of showing off a little of her knowledge. 'Just think of what work it would make of day and night! You see the earth takes 24 hours to turn round on its axis'. . . 'Talking of axes', said the Duchess, 'chop off her head!'"

Lewis Carroll, *Alice in Wonderland*

The image of the Starbucks "progressives" is the image of the pseudo-educated (mostly in critical theory), "politically correct" yuppie Vancouverites who sit drinking over-priced coffee, while they espouse an ideology that more people should be like them and, as the Duchess said, mind their own business. The primary source of their scorn, of course, is the Americans, who, to these progressives, just don't understand that if they could just leave the rest of the world alone, and be tolerant and accommodating like Vancouverites, all would be well. The secondary source of their concern is the suburbanites who live outside the arbitrary boundaries of New City.

In a land where it is always "afternoon", it is always latte time at Starbucks.

For, to the lotos-eater, there is no reason for a "life of toil", just as there is no understanding of a mission to improve the world; and there is no understanding that Starbucks is just another part of lotus land, every bit as much as the beaches of the Gulf Islands, to which these progressives retreat on weekends and summers.

The Starbucks progressive thinks back to when he cut his long hair off in 1972 and decided to go to Teachers' College.   He smiles at the thought of the fixer-upper bungalow he bought in Kitsilano for $85,000 in 1975 and how it is now worth $1,300,000.   He is grateful to Crazy Uncle Lou who left him in his will that cabin near Whaling Station Beach on Hornby Island.   It worked out well because that was the same year he took early retirement from the School Board, so he had time to renovate the place, so now it has been appraised for $750,000.

The Starbucks progressive, living in Kitsilano, Dunbar or Kerrisdale, can ride his bicycle to work at UBC or City Hall, or he runs his consulting practice or artist's studio from his home.   He scorns the suburban types whose polluting cars are stuck in traffic trying to get from their more affordable suburban housing to wherever they work. He supports "Eco-density" as long as it does not appear on his block, and he never stops to ask whether the eco-dense housing will really be built close to where people are actually going to work.

The Starbucks progressive will proudly state that Vancouver does not have any expressways, not understanding that there is no longer any real difference between Vancouver, and Burnaby, Surrey, Richmond and beyond, where there are clogged highways.   It is all Metro Vancouver, and the Starbucks progressive just doesn't understand that because he "got in early" to the real estate market, that is the reason for his superiority to the suburban animal.

Moreover, he is completely confused about the *reason* Vancouver has no expressways.   He assumes it is because of brilliant people like himself making progressive decisions. What he doesn't know is what *The Vancouver Sun's* John Mackie pointed out in an article on January 19, 2008: in the 1950s and '60s there were detailed plans to put freeways through and around Downtown Vancouver. Some were six lanes wide, some would have been "ocean parkways" running right along the ocean. While the plans invariably aroused vocal opposition, Mackie writes that heritage expert John Atkin argues that "the deciding factor was probably the bickering between the federal and provincial governments over who would pay for the freeway system."

Atkins says the federal government finally had enough of the bickering and withdrew from the project. He states: "There's a total reinvention of history going on within the world of early politicos in Vancouver: They talk about how Vancouver made the decision not to have a freeway. Well, no. If the feds and the province had agreed, we would have had a waterfront freeway."

Not living in the suburbs, the Starbucks progressive doesn't care about the actual conditions on the Sky Train rapid transit system, being mainly interested that it not cost too much for the Vancouver taxpayers. In order to keep costs down, we have a bizarre system, where there is no controlled gated entry to enforce the payment of fares, no ticket-sellers/takers, and no drivers on this automated system. Ask any of the ladies who take the Sky Train to and from Surrey how safe they feel as they travel on this system which has only periodic supervision by real people. Ask how they feel to share the Sky Train cars with drunks and drugged-out people who do not bother to pay the same fare that they do. The lovely lady who cuts my hair on West Broadway, and makes the trip in from Surrey has told me the scare stories about what she and her daughter put up with from fellow drunk and drug-taking passengers.

The Starbucks progressive doesn't care about the public transit experience for the hairstylists and restaurant workers who commute from Surrey any more than he cares to have housing for them anywhere in Vancouver. The automated, elevated Skytrain cost three times what it would have cost for a light rail system. Accordingly, for the same money, three times the area could have had rapid transit. The Starbucks progressive is not too interested, as long as he does not have to contribute any of the money. Actually, the reason that there is such an expensive system in place, and it is of such limited coverage, according to *The Vancouver Sun*'s John Mackie, is that the federal government in the run-up to Expo 68 kicked in a lot of money provided that the Skytrain system, built by an Ontario company, would be used. Accordingly, as long as somebody else pays, the Starbucks progressive cares little about what type of housing is built downtown or what type of transit system serves the suburbs. The important thing is that *his* taxes are not raised to pay for it and *his* property value continues to go up.

The Starbucks progressive has read both books by Naomi Klein, most of Noam Chomsky, and has not missed one of Michael Moore's movies. He accepts that for every militant (the word "terrorist" not being politically correct), there is a root cause in some action, or words, of the United States or Israel.

The Starbucks progressive reads his *Georgia Straight* newspaper, so he can stay current with the Arts scene. He gets his international perspective by reading in the *Straight* that clever former Newfoundlander (turned London sophisticate) Gwynne Dyer, since, after all, it says that Dyer's column is published in 175 papers in 45 countries. If he appeals to those in 45 countries, he is obviously saying the right (anti-American) things.

The Starbucks progressive worships the Lotos of nature. The great temple is Stanley Park, and the Starbucks progressive sees the biggest calamity in recent Vancouver history as the day in December 2006 that gale force winds knocked down over 3000 trees, out of an estimated half-million in the 1000-acre park.

"It's an icon, it's so much a part of the identity of Vancouver," Patrick Mooney, a University of British Columbia landscape architecture professor, told CTV.ca about the park.

"It's not really true, but in our minds, it's a big piece of wilderness downtown ... It has everything to do with making this place unique in the world."

Again, it is all about appearances, about our image to the world. But it is more than that. It is a temple, being worshipped:

"People were devastated. They saw the damage and they were crying," Ian Robertson, chairman of the Vancouver Park Board, told CTV.ca.

It took a University of Toronto forestry expert to give some perspective to the grieving Vancouverites, in the same CTV interview. Andy Kenney, an urban forestry expert at the University of Toronto, had some thoughts about the Vancouver situation:

For one thing, what happened in Stanley Park and the others is a normal process in the life of forests, even urban ones, he said.

"That's the thing about these parks. We expect them to have a certain appearance or provide certain benefits to us in perpetuity," Andy Kenney told CTV.ca. "So that whole natural process of disturbance doesn't sit so well, even though it's an ecological reality."

Then, there is that special park, which is probably the world's largest nudist beach within a city limits – Wreck Beach. Vancouver author, Carellin Brooks, has recently written a book about that nudist paradise, next to the University of British Columbia. In her publisher's promotional material for the book, Carellin explains that after she returned from studies in England,

"she rediscovered what it was that had intrigued her about the beach in the first place: the unbridled idealism nestled within its natural beauty. Wreck Beach is one of Vancouver's least commercialized beaches, where concession stands, manmade swimming pools and toilets with plumbing are nothing more than myths. It is this fantastic purity that continues to fascinate her, she says. The first time Brooks shed her clothes and swam in the nude, she recalls, was a 'mystical experience. The day was perfect, sunny, glowing. It was heaven.' Going to the

143

beach is a respite from the fast–paced, commercial lifestyle that's packaged and sold to us daily. Lying in the hot sun, cooling off in the refreshing ocean, reliving the utopian moment of serenity, celebrating the landscape: these are only some of the experiences that she says whisk one's soul away from the chaos of city life."

The Starbucks progressive wants corporations to pay more taxes, but if the property taxes on his $1.5 million West side of Vancouver house go up by 5% to fund affordable housing programs in Vancouver, he will lead a taxpayer's revolt.

As long as the Starbucks progressive has good public transit in his area, he is not in favour of higher taxes to extend it to the suburbanites. He agrees with the Provincial Government that there is not enough density in the Fraser Valley to extend the rapid transit system there. It never occurs to him that rapid transit will promote density, not the other way around. Why would any developer build dense and affordable housing in the suburban towns if there is no public transit? First, the transit line must be started, and then the development will grow around every transit stop. The Starbucks progressive, believing Vancouverites to be a superior life form, doesn't much want his provincial taxes to go to help the others get to work faster.

The Starbucks progressive is big on environmentalism, *as long as somebody else pays for it.* He thinks all new buildings should be "green" according to the LEED program, and of course the costs can be passed along to the buyers/tenants. He thinks that industry can do more to cut greenhouse gases, but personally he doesn't think too much about his frequent airline travel.

The astounding thing about environmentalism in Vancouver is that it focuses on logging companies, global warming, the commuters from the suburbs, and everything where somebody else can be criticized. When it comes to the most elementary form of environmental pollution – sewage treatment and discharge into the ocean - the Starbucks progressives have chosen not to have their tax dollars used for modern clean technologies.

The amazing thing about Vancouver is that the two largest sewage treatment plants are only treating effluent to the primary level, not the secondary level, therefore pumping pollution into the ocean. According to a submission in 2006 by the environmental group, The Georgia Strait Alliance, the key facts regarding *secondary* sewage treatment is that:

- It removes 99% of PCBs and 90% of endocrine disrupting chemicals from the effluent.
- It is the minimum standard in both the United States and the European Union. The current standards in the GVRD, where the two largest treatment plants are only treating at the primary level, places this region far behind a large percentage of the Western world.

According to the Alliance: "Therefore, the GVRD must not only rely on source control for improvements to sewage treatment, but must also commit to upgrading Iona and Lions Gate (sewage treatment plants) to secondary treatment levels today – not in 15 to 20 years. The GVRD must also hasten the replacement of CSOs (combined sewer overflows) and other sources of raw sewage entering our environment."

One wonders what is in the fish that shouldn't be if we had proper sewage treatment. Moreover, as The Georgia Strait Alliance has pointed out, European cities are way ahead of us in resource recovery from sewage – there are over 3500 plants in Europe creating bio-gas from sewage. Sweden runs 5,300 vehicles and much of its transit system on biogas.

As the Alliance states in its 2006 submission to the Waste Management Committee of the former Greater Vancouver Regional District:

"With the majority of the world coming to this region in less than 4 years for the Olympics, our current approach to environmental protection from municipal sewage will be under the microscope and will be difficult to defend. We recognize that upgrades to traditional sewage treatment plants are not inexpensive, however, today we have an opportunity to not only upgrade our treatment levels, but also showcase Greater Vancouver to the world as a sustainable region through the use of new treatment technologies that include resource recovery.

"Sewage treatment plants designed for resource recovery are less expensive to build and operate (more compact, require less electricity and chemicals) than traditional aerobic plants."

So, in the hometown of David Suzuki, our environmentalism may be more for show than anything. We are in favour of environmentalism, but not when it costs *us* any money. When it comes to basic services like sewage disposal, we are a global city allright – a *Third World* global city!

Then, as reported by the *Vancouver Sun* on July 31, 2008, a new federal report had disclosed that with the more extreme weather, including heavier rainstorms, expected as a result of global warming, there will be additional stresses on Vancouver's environmental infrastructure: The heavier rainstorms are expected to frequently overwhelm portions of the region's sewage system, and increase the spilling of raw sewage into Burrard Inlet and the Straight of Georgia.

So just as Beijing has had concerns about the breathability of the air during the 2008 Summer Olympics, Vancouver may have problems with the drinkability of our water during the 2010 Winter Olympics. One hopes not - but the parallels between China using the prestige of the Olympics to cover up its numerous environmental and human rights issues in 2008, and Vancouver using the prestige of its Olympics to cover up its numerous social justice issues are there for all to see.

Another example of our inauthentic environmentalism is that Vancouver residences do not have water meters, and everyone is charged the same flat rate, regardless of use. Of course, there is a financial cost to the installation of water meters, but there is a huge environmental cost to not installing them: there is no inducement to save water, there is no penalty for those who waste water. Of course, this is another example of the Starbucks progressives, while they raised their families and consumed large amounts of water, getting away with forcing the rest of society to subsidize them. We can be sure, that the "boomer" generation of Starbucks progressives, once the children are out of the house, will discover the environmental advantages of water meters – because as they reduce their water use, they will not stand for subsidizing the water use of larger families. Again, it a case of being (or becoming) an environmentalist, as long as somebody else pays.

Then, as of the date of writing this, Metro Vancouver is still considering a plan to truck all of our garbage to Washington State. Environmental progressives who can't even deal with their own garbage can hardly be taken seriously.

Moreover, in our rush to impose environmental costs on new construction of condos (which, as pointed out, elsewhere in this book, helps increase the value of existing real estate), we ignore other basic environmental matters – such as the source of our provincial power. As pointed out by Steve Davis, president of the Independent Power Producers Association of British Columbia, in a *Vancouver Sun* article of January 21, 2008, BC Hydro has reported that almost one in eight houses in B.C. relied on imported power in 2006. He states that most of that power comes from U.S. coal-fired plants that produce a huge amount of greenhouse gas emissions.

What a disconnect between, on the one hand, the tremendous real estate valuations, the stock market holdings, the lucrative pensions, and on the other hand, the reluctance to pay sufficient taxes to take care of the problems in Lotus Land – the Downtown Eastside, the affordability of housing for young people and the entire middle class, the degradation of our ocean by sewage, the failure to deal with our own garbage locally, the eroding health care system, the gangs, and the white collar criminals.

Vancouver is blessed with some wonderful philanthropists, with names like Diamond, Segal, (Milton) Wong, Wosk, Cohen, Barber,

Sauder and many others. Likewise there are some wonderful organizations doing low rent housing, such as The Katherine Sanfield Housing Society (housing mental health patients) and HFBC Housing Foundation (formerly the B.C. Housing Foundation) which concentrates on low rent seniors' housing.

It would be nice if the Starbuck's progressives, with their million dollar homes, would join in a spirit of true progressivism, by accepting higher property taxes, and sharing a little more with the so-called working class. Instead they criticize the perceived lack of morality of the corporate titans, overlooking the fact that such people as Gates, Hilton, and Buffett have given away the majority of their fortunes. Every time that I hear a complaint about property taxes on a $2 million home, all I can think about is the fact that property taxes on a similarly priced home in Vancouver is much lower than most Canadian cities, and that the protestor is actually protesting a modest and elementary form of charity where he or she is being asked to provide some small assistance to other less fortunate members of the community.

In fact, it is not Progressivism that reigns in Vancouver; it is something I choose to call *Tolerism* – an overemphasis on the concept of Tolerance as the supposed highest value of our civilization, and a rejection, like the Mariners, of Good and Evil as measures of morality.

Merriam-Webster defines "tolerance" as:

sympathy or indulgence for beliefs or practices differing from or conflicting with one's own

I think that "sympathy" for the human condition is always a good quality. But what about "indulgence". Merriam-Webster describes the verb "indulging" as:

to give free rein to : to take unrestrained pleasure in :gratify:: to yield to the desire of: to treat with excessive leniency, generosity, or consideration

We should be concerned about the elevation of "tolerance" to the highest value of western civilization, and the extent to which (a) it leaves us open to tolerating what should surely be *intolerable;* and (b) it creates for some reason in its proponents an intolerance to discussing or even hearing any other points of view. The concepts of *political correctness, moral equivalency,* and *moral and cultural relativism* become the ideological blinders for the denizens of the post-religious utopia that narcissistically looks only inward, and not outward to:

1. The need to embrace concrete steps to create social justice in our city;
2. The need to speak out against the terrorism and illiberalism of so many seeking to limit traditional individual human rights with some form of tribal rights, and seeking to limit our rights to even speak out against such measures, since that would be "intolerant".

Of course, Tolerism, as an ideology, is growing all over the country, and in fact all over the Western world, and Europe, in particular. But, in my opinion, Vancouverism reflects most clearly what happens when a Tolerist worldview is applied to local politics. And, living in a Lotus Land, isolated from some of the problems of terrorism that have affected New York, London, Madrid, New Delhi and Tel Aviv, it is of course easy for Vancouverites to lay back on our fine beaches and lecture others about their lack of tolerance. Fortunately, for the Tolerists, our local newspapers in Vancouver seldom bother us with nasty stories of world events on the *front* pages, so that we need not see the distressing headlines as we walk by the newspaper boxes on our sidewalks.

Sometimes I think that the difference between Vancouver and the rest of the country is the difference between Starbucks and Tim Hortons. The Tim Hortons chain, with truly astounding market penetration in the rest of Canada, is now a Canadian icon, more so than the beaver. Of course, Tim Hortons was built on that downscale snack, the donut, and Starbucks does not serve this item of fried dough. (The story of the centrality of the donut shop in the culture of the rest of Canada is now scholarly analyzed in Steve Penfold's *The Donut: A Canadian History*.) Starbucks, the coffee shop of choice in Vancouver, is of course, based in Seattle. Probably, Vancouver has more in common with Seattle, Portland, and San Francisco than with the rest of the country.

Yet as Trevor Boddy has pointed out in "The New Seattle", *Vancouver Magazine,* April 2007, Seattle has the downside of more clogged expressways, and a weaker public domain including lack of public transportation infrastructure. But it has the upside of a vibrant corporate sector, great job opportunities and corporate philanthropy funding many cultural facilities. There are similarities in style, in climate and location, but there is a corporate creation of real wealth that goes beyond real estate and investments.

The Starbucks progressive, because neither he nor his friends work in the corporate world, do not understand the upside of the corporate world, and the appeal of actually developing products for society. According to Boddy:

"Vancouver's core attitude—a sense of God-granted entitlement—twinned with a need for quick returns are our legacies from history, because wealth here was generated by scooping up minerals, knocking down forests and, since 1986, harvesting the last of our non-renewable natural resources: water-view real estate."

If Vancouver's economic history is conceptualized in this way, there are real concerns about the sustainability of the model. Recent increases in the value of the Canadian dollar make our products – lumber, natural gas, and real estate – more expensive to the Americans who are our best customers. The anti-American Starbucks progressive doesn't understand that a declining U.S. economy will eventually send economic shockwaves, the extent of which are quite unknown.

The Starbucks progressive didn't see the problem in rezoning most of Downtown Vancouver to residential from offices, because he thinks that corporations are immoral and we can do without them. It is not surprising that Joel Bakan, author of *The Corporation: The Pathological Pursuit of Profit and Power*, teaches law at Vancouver's University of British Columbia. Of course, the Starbuck's progressive has a difficult time comprehending that *all* organizations of humans, whether they are corporations, non-governmental organizations, or even university faculties, contain the same pathologies in pursuit of power and the money necessary to fund the organization.

As usual, it is easier to blame those organizations of which you are not a member and do not benefit you directly; accordingly anti-corporate blather is centred at universities which *themselves* are pathological in terms of pursuing money and power. The University of British Columbia sits on thousands of acres of prime real estate on a peninsula at the western tip of Vancouver, overlooking the ocean. Portions of the land are being sold off to high-end developers at high prices for the development of high end housing, with the rationale that these are "endowment lands" which must fund the future growth and operating expenses of this vast corporation. Virtually none of it is being devoted to social housing, low income housing, or any type of affordable rental or purchased housing. Vancouver's anti-corporate professors ought to look a bit more in the mirror.

Although I am a critic of the amount of money spent on the 2010 Winter Olympics, I do acknowledge that corporate sponsors are being directed to benefit needy communities. The best example is how the Rona building supply chain, as part of its sponsor obligations, has funded a $3 million dollar program of training 64 at risk younger people in a carpentry apprentice program. This is part of the Winter Games' Inner City Inclusivity agreement, that provides for some economic spin-off to help disadvantaged communities, like the DES. The point is that corporations can be guided into social responsibility, and those who build themselves up by blaming others, should first reflect upon their own social justice credentials.

An anti-corporate bias in land use, of course, as we discuss in Chapter 16, is fine if you are content to become a resort, not a complete city. (Although all the developers of these resorts are corporations, too, and we tend to downplay pathologies that help make us Vancouverites rich.) Boddy writes eloquently of what has happened as a result of this image of the Downtown as a residential district only:

"The net effect of this downtown forest of condo towers is a kind of reverse clear-cut: a single species monoculture plantation for the quick harvesting of profits by politically savvy developers. And with this development, ironically, we may have permanently compromised our most attractive feature—our spectacular natural setting—for future businesses and downtown workers both."

But the Lotos-Eaters of Vancouver have always marched to the beat of a different drummer. Vancouver, as mentioned above, sometimes seems little connected to the rest of Canada. I don't think you can underestimate the gulf that was created, during federal elections, when Vancouverites would turn on their televisions at 8:00 Pacific time, and would find that the national election was already decided, even before the B.C. votes were counted.

And having a mountain range dividing us from the rest of the country is another factor in our feeling of separation.

But, most of all, the Lotos-Eaters feel we can strut our inauthentic environmentalism, our anti-corporatism, and our individualized spirituality - mainly because we have fooled ourselves into believing that we are somehow "progressive", and are "the best place on earth". We sit on the beaches of Lotus Land, congratulating ourselves on our tolerance and for abolishing the concepts of good and evil, and convincing ourselves that money, tranquility, and beauty are the gods of our world. It is this theme that we discuss in Chapter 12.

Chapter 12

The Decline of Religion and the Worship of the Esthetic

Death is the end of life; ah, why
Should life all labour be?
Let us alone. Time driveth onward fast,
And in a little while our lips are dumb.
Let us alone. What is it that will last?
All things are taken from us, and become
Portions and parcels of the dreadful past.
Let us alone. What pleasure can we have
To war with evil? Is there any peace
In ever climbing up the climbing wave?
All things have rest, and ripen toward the grave
In silence; ripen, fall and cease:
Give us long rest or death, dark death, or dreamful ease.

How sweet it were, hearing the downward stream,
With half-shut eyes ever to seem
Falling asleep in a half-dream!
To dream and dream, like yonder amber light,
Which will not leave the myrrh-bush on the height;
To hear each other's whisper'd speech;
Eating the Lotos day by day,
To watch the crisping ripples on the beach,
And tender curving lines of creamy spray;
To lend our hearts and spirits wholly
To the influence of mild-minded melancholy;
To muse and brood and live again in memory,
With those old faces of our infancy
Heap'd over with a mound of grass,
Two handfuls of white dust, shut in an urn of brass!

From "The Lotos Eaters", Alfred Tennyson

"You might be a rock 'n' roll addict prancing on the stage,
You might have drugs at your command, women in a cage,
You may be a business man or some high degree thief,
They may call you Doctor or they may call you Chief

But you're gonna have to serve somebody, yes indeed
You're gonna have to serve somebody,
Well, it may be the devil or it may be the Lord
But you're gonna have to serve somebody. "

-Bob Dylan, "Gotta Serve Somebody", *Slow Train Coming,* 1979.

The Lotos-Eaters reject the notion of Good and Evil, inherent in Religion. They believe that right and wrong can be determined on a case by case basis, not understanding that, in the absence of religion, prevailing ideology becomes the arbiter of right and wrong. Then arguments about ideology end quickly as reassuring yet anachronistic titles of Left and Right are trotted out to quickly slot the other side and quickly end any discussion. The mariners argue that Death is the end of life; that being left alone to their pleasures of the beautiful Lotos land is all that is important, because "there is no joy but calm!" "Sweet music" is lauded, along with the beauty of the "land of streams", its "charmed sunset", the dale seen "thro' mountain clefts" and "many a winding vale (a)nd meadow, set with slender galingale". (Galingale is an aromatic root.)

The Lotos-Eaters still want to categorize people into *Left wing* and *Right wing*, when the categories should be *Tolerists* versus *non-Tolerists*.

Esthetics – beautiful sounds, beautiful sights, beautiful tastes, and beautiful smells are the values of the Lotos-Eaters.

Religion, however, posits an after-life and is based on pursuing Good over Evil. Vancouverites have the lowest participation in organized

154

religion in all of Canada, and also live in what is arguably Canada's most beautiful setting.   Bob Dylan states the position that everyone ends up worshipping someone or something.   In Vancouver, has an *appreciation* for the esthetic passed into a *worship* of the esthetic?

And has the psychological imperative to *know* thyself turned into a cultural self-absorption?   Douglas Todd is the religion writer for *The Vancouver Sun*.   In an astute column published on December 1, 2007, Todd questions whether the image of a "blessed out people lost in themselves" have made "Alternative spirituality" in the Pacific Northwest, not "countercultural", but the "centre" of culture itself.

Todd refers to the "New Age" spiritualists as the "secular but spiritual" crowd, and concludes that since only 40% of the population here follows "institutional" religion, the secular but spiritual folks are the mainstream.   He asks the critical question: Do the secular but spiritual tend towards the "egocentric and self-absorbed"?

He argues that many of those who hate organized religion do so for "reasons related to their upbringings or to global conflicts."   He also argues, and it is hard to disagree, that institutions of a religious nature are valuable because they "can provide a framework for social change."   He quotes Mark Shibley of Southern Oregon University, who remarks on the common belief among secular but spiritual people that if people change their "inner lives", social change will inevitably follow.   Shibley however believes such an approach leaves out the whole question of what "strategy" will then be adopted to transform inner spirituality into social justice.

And the data seems to back up Professor Shibley. Todd cites a poll by Andrew Greenville of Angus Reid polling firm in Canada that summed up some of the constituent values of secular but sprirtual anti-religion: the survey, according to Todd's article, showed that people in the Pacific Northwest "strongly emphasize private experiences of the sacred, don't worry as much about the gap between the wealthy and the poor, and are less interested in politics"

Todd puts it so well: "They revere the wilderness, tasting the Garden of Eden, while hiking or skiing. They experience wilderness as sacred, a cathedral. The downside of such nature spirituality is romanticism, wanting to preserve the wilderness while virtually writing off profane cities, where most humans live."

This explains the near worship of parkland in Vancouver. The loss of trees in Stanley Park during the windstorm of December, 2006 resulted in the public raising some $2.2 million for remediation, along with a charitable gift of $1 million by prominent local businessman, Jimmy Pattison.

The very notion of parkland is different in Vancouver than elsewhere. Parkland, in most places, is seen as having several functions – the preservation and conservation of nature and natural ecosystems, a place for appropriate types of sports, and a place for *recreation* (in the widest sense) for urban masses who live in dense housing without their own backyards and access to grass, flowers, etc.

However, the Park Board and Park bureaucrats in Vancouver have added a new more important purpose to parks, and raised it to a quasi-religious dictate – the pursuit of beauty. The best way to understand this is to look at what has happened to the design, construction and cost of community centres, those formerly utilitarian buildings, used by community gatherings, education, and recreation. In Vancouver, as Frances Bula, has written in the December 22, 2007 edition of *The Vancouver Sun*, there is a philosophy of "Community Centre Beautiful" since the 1990s, with more than half a dozen centres, pools and rinks, finished or under construction, that are "works of modern art."

She quotes Piet Rutgers, the park board's chief planner: "The pursuit of beauty is part of what the parks are all about. And these community centres are basically the living rooms of the community. So we want to make them beautiful." Of course, hiring the most talent architects comes at a price, and even if they modify their usual high fees, the construction of iconic structures with curves, special glass, and unusual rooflines, all costs extra money, in a city that so

156

neglects its lower income population in terms of basic matters of housing and transportation.

Never mind the expense. In a land deficient of the kind of big corporations which are usually the source of gorgeous architecture commissions, the parks board has committed the public purse to this purpose: Says the Park Board's project manager, Rudy Roelefson, "It's been our objective to get the best architects. We want them." In her article, Bula states: "the park board has seasoned planners, architects and engineers on staff who like and promote good design… the park board is willing to spend the extra money to build their designs, which don't come at bargain prices." In her article, this "enlightened" attitude is contrasted to the "different mindset" of B.C. Housing, where one architect states of their social housing projects: "it's got to be durable and it can be nice, but not too nice because there's a perception you're throwing money away."

And so, even though Vancouver has the beauty, both natural and man-made, of the huge Stanley Park, there is a push for more beauty, no matter the cost. In May, 2008, the VanDusen Botanical Garden, a 22-hectare show garden at Oak and 37th, unveiled plans to spend $20 million on renovations, including a state-of-the-art architectural masterpiece for administration and education. The new building will have a stylish petal-shaped roof, inspired by an orchid flower, and this undulating five-petal roof will, of course, be partly "green" – having a covering of plants. Other green aspects will consist of solar-powered hot water, collection of rain water, and recycled "grey water" for irrigation.
As well, there will be two new restaurants, one formal and one casual.

So, Vancouverism sees nothing wrong with spending another $20 million (or more) on more beauty in the parks, at the same time there is an outright crisis in affordable housing. The same $20 million could be given as inducements to the private sector to obtain a dozen or more affordable rental buildings.

(It is culturally and politically significant that in Vancouver, a term or two on the Parks Board is considered a stepping-stone to running for a seat on City Council.)

Fortunately, there is one community centre being planned, that working people can relate to – the new Mount Pleasant Community Centre will have rental apartments in its upper floors.   This is the model so desperately needed: In an era where there is a crisis in affordable housing, high end, costly works of art, in the guise of community centres and parkland buildings, are a result of confused thinking.   But just as our traditional Churches built magnificent structures of the highest design and material quality in their day, so too does their modern equivalent – the Park Board – erect church-like monuments to the god of beauty.   It is only when we *worship the esthetic aspect of parks*, can we become so confused as a culture that we spend extra millions of dollars, when our young and working class cannot afford to live here.

There is, to be sure, a fundamental conflict in the minds and hearts of those who live in cities yet "worship" nature.   That is why the promotion of *density* by the large developers who profit the most by it, has met such a welcome reception – we are psychologically predisposed to welcome the idea that building dense towers will reduce our footprint in nature. Perhaps the innate insecurity of our belief in that proposition, conduces to the narcissism that then brags that we have constructed the "best place on earth."   But the better the place is, the more tourists and part time residents and full time residents we shall attract, thus harming what we purport to value most about the place.

Of course, those of us who preached for years about the necessity for density to avoid suburban sprawl, have now discovered that the developers of luxury high rises are now finding great profit in the confluence of design-pride and the as-yet unrefined philosophy of density at any cost.   By this I mean that vast areas of expensive real estate are being created where it is deemed appropriate for 50 story buildings, which are then surrounded by older suburbs, then newer suburbs all catering to those who want their space.   Sophisticates are saying, as was stated in a November 2007 *Toronto Star* article by Christopher Hume, that "height is right". The article's lead-in says: "With more than 150 condo projects on the books, Toronto is growing up fast. Height, it seems is the new religion in urban planning. That's a good thing."

In the Hume article, Toronto's acting chief planner, Gary Wright, states: "We're not afraid of height...What matters is the pedestrian experience and the building's relationship with the street."

In this "religion" celebrating the esthetic relationship of the building and the street, is there room for a discussion of where people should live, which family sizes should live where, what income levels should live where, and how do we create a *just* city, and not just an *esthetically pleasing* front yard to impress our guests?

(Vancouver social worker Abba Brodt once pointed out to me the symbolism inherent in Vancouver houses having beautiful front yards and porches to show the world, while the more private space is taken up by sometimes decrepit garages, laneways, and large garbage bins, which are visited regularly by unemployed "binners" with their shopping carts, looking for recyclables or other goods that can be sold, to bring them a little money.)

And in Vancouver is there an overemphasis on design to the detriment of good building practices? There are many cases of leaky condos where the developer was importing a "southwestern" design from California, with extensive use of stucco, which failed to meet basic standards for prevention of water leakage into the units. There is a good case to argue that overall some of the fanciest designs create some of the biggest problems. A *just* city and province would have sufficient laws to protect the owners of now leaky condos from the developers, architects and engineers that caused the problems for them.

When I first moved to Vancouver, I heard a lot about UBC's Museum of Anthropology, designed by famous local architect Arthur Erickson. In June, 2006, there was a program taking place there where famous architects from around the world were giving their impressions of architecture in their own cities, and then their impressions after a quick tour of Vancouver. The program was called, "Dialogue of Cities - Public Dialogue: Vancouver Viewed and Reviewed".

Some of the best minds in Architecture were there, representing cities such as New York, London, Rome, Mexico City, Nairobi, Havana, Hong Kong and Dubai.

I was quite interested to go to the program;   firstly, to see the architectural gem, and secondly to hear the reaction of international architects to what they had seen.

The event took place in the Great Hall, with its massive 15 metre tall glass wall facing the beautiful ocean and mountain vistas to the west. The program started with a reception at 5:30 and the speakers started at 6:00, on this beautiful sunny early summer Vancouver day.

There were, alas, several problems with the event. Although this was a clear departure from the normal inward looking narcissism of Vancouver elites, the architects brought in to speak only had a short time to look around the City.   Even still, they were able to quickly vocalize the major problems, although it may be that their criticisms were somewhat modified by a reluctance to be rude to their hosts. (Notes   taken   in   part   from   Richard   Eriksson   at **www.urbanvancouver.com/node/4016**):

Louise Noelle Gras from Mexico City stated that it being her first time in Vancouver, she was impressed with the natural scenery (the flowers, the mountains, the sea), but was very strongly negative about what she perceived as Vancouver's "condo craze" (a phrase repeated by other critics) and "foolish greediness". She worried that, even though it was a small part of Vancouver, it could grow into something bigger.

Robert Segre, who divides his time between Havana and Rio de Janeiro, was sad about the amount of towers and condos, as the towers fight between each other for views of the surrounding landscape.

Towers, he said, were not the only way to keep people in the city: parks and urban spaces could do that as well. He is worried about the lack of space between each tower, and that they are often empty, with people from Asia buying them up in case things go bad in their home country and they have to suddenly move to North America.

Samia Rab from Dubai noticed that during the work day the streets were largely empty, and hence not that different from many other city centres, and noted that towers not only frame the views of the water, but our relationship to the surrounding landscape. The challenges Vancouver faces, she said, include how to merge public interests with private interests (she noted that Robson St. was essentially an outdoor mall), and making tourism not the economy—as she says it is not a viable economy—but **part** of the economy. She reiterated that architects design space to be occupied by *people* (who make it a place).

Dennis Sharp from London asked us to consider a city of views, that is, to the things beyond the thing we're looking at. Vancouver has very much glass architecture, and when more towers get built in glass, the position of glass towers in relation to each other matters. He then asked if there was a master plan for Vancouver, whether the towers meet housing requirements for students and those with low-incomes, etc.

Desmond Hui from Hong Kong, while critical of the Downtown "condo craze" was impressed by the Central City project in Surrey. He suggested that Hong Kong developers might be a cause for the excessive height of condos. He brought a perspective from Hong Kong, where he cited statistics that in Hong Kong, there were 7 square meters per person on the island city, and only 20% of the land is "buildable". He then argued that since Vancouver has a lot more land than Hong Kong, Vancouver has more options than building up, to the same height as Hong Kong towers.

And so, the audience heard some clear challenges to our Vancouverism.

The second problem with the event, oddly enough, had to do with the "stunning" architecture of the "world famous" Arthur Erickson-designed Museum of Anthropology (now undergoing an expansion of 50% more space at a cost of approximately $52 million). You see, with its huge 15 metre wall of glass facing southwest, and an event taking place at 6:00 in early June, there is a problem on a sunny day. The sun, beginning to set in the west comes shining full-blast into the auditorium. I estimate that the temperature inside was about 10 to 15 degrees Celsius higher than outside. There are no shades, and no air conditioning.

People "in the know' had seemed to take all the seats on the far left and far right of the auditorium, because they were in the shade. The rest of us, baking in the sun, sweated our way through the talks, leaving me, unfortunately, only one lasting impression of this "stunning" architecture – the stunning lack of concern for those who would be using the building, at a certain time of day. I know that is not an entirely fair criticism of a building with so many other great design features, but unfortunately that is all I can remember about the inside of the building.

Another thing I remember is highly regarded Vancouver architect Bing Thom standing up in the question period and saying he wanted to get people to talk about transportation and authenticity, as Vancouver was once a colonial city for the British, and is now in some ways for Asia. If it's going to go from a port city to a service city, stated Thom, how do we find our authenticity? I kept thinking to myself, it is better to raise that late (i.e. in 2006), than never. Maybe a waterfront turned over almost entirely to condos is *inauthentic*?

Thom's remarks seemed critical to me. I know very well that for an architect as intellectual as Thom, the notion of "authenticity" implies not just genuineness to tradition, but rather an esthetic good, unto itself. For me, however, with my interest in the connection between ideology and public policy, "authenticity" implies a genuineness to the *best values* of tradition, not just the surface aspects of tradition. And to me, improved policies based upon improved values trump esthetics every time.   However, I acknowledge those who value authenticity simply for its link to local tradition.

This takes us to one of the best novels about Vancouver written in the last ten years, Timothy Taylor's exquisitely written *Stanley Park* (Vintage Canada, 2001).   Taylor's protagonist, Jeremy Papier, freshly back from a school for chefs in France, opens a Vancouver restaurant specializing in locally sourced foods.   At the same time, Jeremy's father, a semi-retired Professor of Anthropology is researching the work to be the great culmination of his career – a study of the homeless living in Stanley Park – and he chooses to live among the homeless.   As the Professor says (at page 136), implicitly linking his son's work as a chef using local ingredients to his own anthropology of the homeless denizens of Stanley Park:

" It's about roots and place. It's about how people relate to the land on which they stand. In our rootless day and age, our time of strange cultural homelessness – and worse, our social amnesia about what used to constitute both the rewards and limitations of those roots – I wonder if we might look to these homeless… to find an emblem of the deepest roots of all."

Alas, Chef Jeremy's restaurant runs into financial difficulties through his financial mis-management; his food, however, is so good that it attracts the attention of the owner of a chain of Starbucks-like coffee houses, who buys out 95% of Jeremy's restaurant, saving Jeremy's job, but leaving Jeremy a mere cog in a part of a mega-business that must be run by sound business decisions, one of which is to drop the emphasis on local sourcing, in favour of esoteric foods from around the world.   Jeremy loses his soul, but rather than admit defeat, he relishes the chance to create the most original and unheard-of Vancouver fare, served with dashing esthetics and originality.

Jeremy and his staff hit a gastronomical home-run with their opening-night extravaganza. Yet, the inclusion of rarely served meats and fowl from around the world, creates a backlash from animal rights' activists, and plants a doubt in the corporate owner that Jeremy's creations are too unique; in seeking the links between *all animals* and *all soils*, he has tested the upper limits of Vancouver's tolerance for the unique and the world-class; Jeremy is fired, and starts over again in his own small restaurant.

Jeremy's father, while studying the homeless in Stanley Park, adopts a diet of barbecued squirrel, birds and ducks, caught in the Park. While somewhat estranged from his father at the beginning of the book, Jeremy and his father bridge their differences as Jeremy gives his father (and a cast of other homeless characters) the benefit of his expert preparation and sauces for the free park fare. At the same time, his girlfriend, also working for the large corporation finds some squirrel in the freezer at Jeremy's apartment, which she mentions to others, which helps facilitate Jeremy's downfall.

So, Taylor effectively asks in *Stanley Park*: how seriously do we and should we take our roots and our authenticity? How fast do the generation Xers and Yers sell out when a corporation offers to buy their ideas? Are we in fact seeking not authenticity, but *experience* – a need for an ever broader array of foods, travel experiences, and esthetic experiences as we flit from one trend to another?

Stanley Park can be read many ways, probably all rewarding. But the questions posed about Vancouver's fundamental authenticity, and the notion that the homeless in Stanley Park may be more authentic than anyone, answer quite profoundly Bing Thom's question about Vancouver architecture and authenticity. To me, the sell-out of local values to the international experience, whether it be back-packing around the world, smoking dope as you go, international business, or limiting yourself to gastronomic tourism in Vancouver's excellent restaurants, is ultimately morally unsatisfying. Experience without values is an animalistic pastime.

The problem, however, is that I know that in Vancouver mine is a minority position. Not only is the esthetic the ideal, not only is the esthetic the link to genuine and authentic tradition, but it has become one of the few agreed upon goals in itself, in our "secular-but-spiritual" culture. In that sense, the Lotos-Eaters worship Esthetics, as well as Nature, and that is certainly clear from Tennyson, just as it is clear from the tears shed when Vancouver suffered the loss of trees in Stanley Park. So, in addition to esthetics, the Lotos-Eaters worship Nature, and that is a problem for city-dwellers. The Lotos-Eaters never stopped to realize, then, that when they landed in paradise, the mere fact of staying there diminished that very paradise, no matter what alternative esthetics they were able to create.

I worry that with the adoption of "spirituality" devoid of *values* instead of the fixed moral values inherent in traditional "religious" teachings, the mariners' goal of a carefree and relaxed existence will continue to predominate in Lotus Land. But Tennyson's poem forces us to ask whether people can truly be happy without the challenge of making the world a better place, and the challenge of aspiring to personal greatness.

There is nothing wrong with *feeling* good and *looking* good, but religion, at its best, inspires us in *doing* good.

It is high time for a wide-ranging debate about balancing esthetics and social justice within the spirituality of Lotus Land.

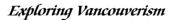

Chapter 13

The Original "Mild-eyed" Lotos-Eaters:
Respecting and Accommodating Aboriginal Rights

"And round about the keel with faces pale,
Dark faces pale against that rosy flame,
The mild-eyed melancholy Lotos-eaters came.
Branches they bore of that enchanted stem,
Laden with flower and fruit, whereof they gave
To each"

- Afred Tennyson, "The Lotos-Eaters"

Thus far in our exploration of Vancouverism, we seem to have stressed the negative aspects of the Lotus Land as ideological foundation for Vancouverism.

In this chapter, however, we look at one of the bright spots of this foundation for Vancouverism, specifically the respect and accommodation directed to aboriginals, who in the ideology of Lotus Land, represent the "mild-eyed melancholy Lotos-eaters" who brought the mariners the "enchanted stem", and thus welcomed them to paradise.

As Tennyson notes, in the "rosy flame" of the spectacular sunsets over the ocean, "dark faces pale against the rosy flame". Sharing the lotos and sharing the beauty caused the mariners to see the aboriginals not as *dark-skinned* "others", but in fact as *pale-skinned* like themselves, in the light of the setting sun, sharing the enchanted lotos fruit.

If Real Estate is King in Vancouver, and the mild-eyed melancholy Lotos-eaters were good enough to share the Lotos, then the newer Vancouverites understood that the Real Estate would have to be shared with the First Nations. This aberration in the usual selfishness and greed of Vancouverism is so stark and exceptional, that only such an analysis can help clarify its exceptionality.

This is not meant to explain the early history of British Columbia, where actions against aboriginals were little different than in the rest of Canada. But it is meant to explain more recent developments, led by Premier Gordon Campbell of British Columbia, to forge a "new relationship" with the First Nations.

And this is not meant to discuss the sad situation of so many "urban aboriginals", being those who have left reserves for the big city of Vancouver, hoping for jobs, education and decent accommodation, and finding instead poor health, lack of child care and good-paying jobs, and lack of affordable housing. Vancouver is home to some 40,000 aboriginals, having the third largest aboriginal population of any city in Canada (behind only Winnipeg and Edmonton). Aboriginal children are twice as likely to be raised in single-parent families as non-aboriginal children. Aboriginals make up five percent of the total provincial population in British Columbia and nearly 2% of Vancouver's population.

Instead, we shall focus on two recent land claims settlements, one near the suburban town of Tsawwassen, and one in the prime Vancouver neighbourhood of Point Grey, adjacent to the University of British Columbia. The first was a comprehensive treaty, and thus preferable to the second, which was a type of interim land settlement, leaving future claims outstanding.

In the summer of 2007, 130 of the 187 registered voters of the Tsawwassen First Nation ratified a treaty with the British Columbia government, about which said Chief Kim Baird:

"More land, cash and resources provide us the opportunity to create a healthy and viable community, free from the constraints of the Indian Act. We now have the tools to operate as a self-governing nation, for the first time in 150 years.

"Our ancestors have been honoured. And our children and future generations will be proud of the treaty made by our community."

This 358 person band, of whom approximately half live on a reserve and half off the reserve, spent 14 years in negotiations and the treaty making process. Finally, an agreement ended the status of the Reserve system and gave the band full ownership rights. They are receiving full ownership of 372 hectares of former provincial Crown land, 290 ha. of former Indian reserve land, and 62 ha. of land which, while owned by the band, will be under the jurisdiction of the municipality of Delta.

The Tsawwassen First Nation is receiving a capital transfer of some $13 million, with a commitment that every five years a fiscal financing agreement will be negotiated to fund programs and services. It will have authority to tax its members living on treaty lands; the Province will share 50% of provincial income tax and sales tax revenue collected from the members who are on the lands, and it will also transfer 100% of property taxes collected from anyone living on treaty lands.

In terms of government, the treaty provides for democratic government with a constitution, subject to the Canadian Constitution and Charter of Rights and Freedoms. The Tsawwassen First Nation will become a member of Metro Vancouver and will appoint a director to its board. The Tsawwassen First Nation will have powers similar to other municipal governments regarding land-use planning, traffic regulation, fire protection and public works.

When one considers the time, expense and energy that went into this treaty, and the obligations thereunder by all concerned, it boggles the mind, especially when one considers that the band consists at present of 358 people. While it boggles the mind, it also should be a source of pride for all concerned at the extent to which the provincial government has gone to provide social and economic opportunities, legal certainties and most of all to remedy past wrongs in a manner which should provide a better future.

While the Tsawwassen First Nation resides in a mixed urban and agricultural area near the Tsawwassen Ferry Terminal, the 1,000 member Musqueam First Nation reside right in the middle of some of Vancouver's priciest real estate, on the west side near the University of British Columbia. In fact, the Musqueam once considered most of what is now Vancouver their nation, and it was sadly typical that they were forced into a tiny reserve. However, with Premier Gordon Campbell's "new relationship", the Musqueam have now been given 88 hectares of prime real estate, including the U.B.C. golf course, and including 8.5 hectares out of the adjacent Pacific Spirit Park, of which development will be permitted on 7.3 ha.

The biggest downside to the Musqueam settlement is that legally it is just a settlement of some outstanding court claims, rather than a comprehensive treaty. The Musqueam continue to have other claims throughout parts of Vancouver and the Lower Mainland. While a comprehensive treaty would have been better, at least some immediate cash and developable land will be given to the Musqueam now (assuming the settlement is ratified in early 2008), and the Musqueam need that.

In a column in *The Vancouver Sun* on November 26, 2007, Miro Cernetig estimated that the total Musqueam land package, given Vancouver's real estate prices, could be worth as much as $1 billion.

To be sure, there is a continuing conflict, not even close to being resolved, between large forestry companies and native bands over logging rights. Perhaps that is because these disputes, most often in the north-central part of the province, are not really involving the parties who reside in the actual Lotus Land of the Lower Mainland. Time will tell.

Furthermore, the aboriginals who are most visible, in that they live closest to Vancouver, seem to have an advantage over those who live farther into the interior. In many out of the way locations, aboriginals live in truly deplorable situations, with substandard housing, almost impassable roads through the forest, and in some cases are unconnected to the electrical power grid, and therefore reliant on dirty diesel generators.

However, in Lotus Land, itself, the mild eyed Lotos Eaters are given more respect than elsewhere. Now we understand why the UBC Museum of Anthropology, filled with Aboriginal artifacts, is given so much money for expansion. And why the city's most esteemed architect is given the architectural commission. Instinctively, we know who was here first, and our political culture reflects that knowledge.

All this means that the ideology of Lotus Land makes us prepared to extend benefits eventually to most Aboriginals. It does seem that in Lotus Land we are ahead of other places in Canada with respect to a generous accommodation to overcome historical wrongs. In Lotus Land, there has occurred the realization that the "mild-eyed Lotos-eaters" got to this paradise first, and therefore must be compensated. It is one part of Vancouverism that does represent the best in social justice.

Chapter 14

The Lotus Land of the Sky:
Architecture and Social Justice

"The operative point of view for designers … becomes one of empathy for the human condition."

- Robert Ivy, FAIA and Editor, *Architectural Record*, in the Foreword to the *Universal Design Handbook*

The built form of a city obviously has social effects, as well as technical architectural effects. In this chapter, we think about the relationship between Vancouver's evolving built form and issues of social justice.

"Social Justice" is somewhat of a contentious term, with some conservative writers objecting to the connotation of equality of result, as opposed to the extension of merciful caring. I simply use the term as reflective of a mindset that wishes to extend the benefits of our wealth and assets in this "livable city" to a greater number of people. I will leave it to others to refine the norms and objectives.

I sympathize with those who advocate "compassionate conservatism" which is a term reflective of a mindset which, in the contest of preserving the present politico-economic system, wishes to extend compassion to those who are needy in one way or another.

What can we say about the "Vancouver model" of architecture and its effect on social justice? This is not often talked about, in the narrow terms of architecture. But surely this is a matter deserving of consideration, and what follows are a few of the issues.

Firstly, we should consider that removal of the individual from the community makes it less likely that the individual will care about the social issues of the community. Removal from the community can be "actual" or "constructive". For example, in certain Latin American cities where crime is rampant in the shanty towns in certain areas, the well-to-do live in homes protected by large concrete, stone or iron walls, with secure gates. Being able to hide in these individual "fortresses", to my mind, conduces to a disconnectedness to the reality of the social problems existing outside the fortress. This is a "constructive" removal from the community.

Likewise, in certain areas of the world, the rich have estates, with guard-houses to screen all visitors.

In fact, the "Vancouver model" of downtown high-end condos accomplishes the same thing, with the guard-houses and walls replaced by a concierge and security personnel. A vertical distance shields the residents from the realities of the street below. Secure in an upscale box in the sky, looking out at mountain views and the shimmering blue ocean, the occupant is removed from the community below - into the Lotus Land of the Sky.

As we discuss elsewhere, the preeminence of the esthetic in Vancouverism blinds us to other values. We are proud of how the Vancouver Model places slim high rises on "podiums" of townhouses or retail development, thereby creating a more friendly face to the street, rather than having a high rise move up in the sky directly from the edge of the sidewalk, cutting off light, and creating more wind tunnels. But too many architecture critics have too narrow a focus. Toronto has a very active program of luxury high rises being built in its downtown, as it seems to be following the Vancouver Model. But the *Toronto Star's* Urban Affairs Columnist, Christopher Hume, writing on November 17, 2007, in an article entitled "Vertical Village", waxes enthusiastically about height and good design, as Toronto has more than 10 buildings underway with heights in excess of 50 stories and 160 metres:

"Indeed the real issue is not height, but design, which is to say, how a building relates to its surroundings, what it gives back to the city, and how it meets the street."

May I suggest that the *real* issue is not the building, but the residents to be housed there. Given that density is required, how does the building help the *residents* relate to their surroundings, how does it help the *residents* to give back to the city, and how will they meet the street in terms of connecting to the wider society around them? We are not talking about sculpture, but housing for real people in a dynamic and integrated city.

Of course, downtown Vancouver has wonderful pedestrian opportunites, which includes the fabulous seawall for walking, biking and rollerblading, and includes the high-end shopping of Robson Street. The question of course is whether such walking to amenities is a real connection to a real world, or just another Lotus Land.

We know, for example, that the convenience of high-rise condo living is attractive to part-time residents, and they will of course have less connection to the issues of the community, except as they relate to their community of the strata corporation.

But, what of full-time residents? Surely the built form of a high-rise, with no individualized doorway to the street, having all of your daily relationship with the street filtered through the front desk, affects one's view of where you live, and what encompasses your community. Having your own door (as is the case in most townhouses) to the outside world, without the intermediation by the security personnel, causes a different feeling of connection.

The height and massing of the condo towers conduce to an image of a "global city" as opposed to a small town community, or even as opposed to any concept of living in a "neighbourhood". The self image as international citizen, or even as a national businessman, is counter-productive to identification with local, municipal issues. In this way, I fear that the phrase "world class" city has come to mean identification with a "class" that is not so much "upper" class, but a "transcendent" class, transcending the parochial, local issues. But it is these parochial, local issues – caring for the mentally ill and homeless, creating appropriate housing for your workforce and your young, dealing with crime, drugs, and even local labour relations – that constitute the compassion required of being a "good neighbour". The international, or should I say *supra-national* residents of the towers, in general, care less about being good neighbours, and the nature of their living space contributes to that lack of concern.

I view it as a kind of "Hong Kong" mentality: from their high-rises in Hong Kong, many of the businessmen and women of Hong Kong, interested in international capital and movement of goods and products between China and the rest of the world, managed to transition quite well from British rule to Chinese rule - from a British-type democracy with fundamental freedoms to the rule of China which gives no individual rights, except property rights, and even then, only in the city for the business class, not in the rural areas to farmers.

Time magazine in November of 2007 had a feature story about upwardly mobile young Chinese in the large cities of China, and how they are interested in all the yuppie toys, but are quite willing to stay silent on issues of politics and liberal justice. Surely, the separation from the community on the street, which comes with the architectural form of choice, makes easier this sad duality between business success and social disengagement.

Larry Beasley, the former Vancouver co-director of Planning, is a dynamic and talented planner who is widely viewed as instrumental in the construction of the "Vancouver model. At the end of October, 2007, he spoke at McGill University in Montreal, on the topic, "Making a Great City by Design". The urban planning professor at McGill, who invited Beasley to lecture, Raphael Fischler, made this evaluation of Beasley's legacy:

"He looked at urban design as a city-building strategy. It has to do with the aesthetic and the cosmetic, but it's much more than that. It's about shaping a place where people live and work and play. Place-making is an important element and Vancouver has made that kind of achievement."

Allright, urban design is about "place-making", but I wish the good professor would do something other than state the obvious.   What kind of place are we making, and for whom are we making it?   Again, while Beasley accomplished much, it must be asked: Are working people, young people, and people with young children happy about the place that was created?   Who gets to decide what kind of place is being created?   Planners, of course, should be implementing the vision of the Municipal Councils that employ them.   What was the vision of the Vancouver council?   Beasley himself has now starting re-thinking these matters, and as an Adjunct Professor at UBC's School of Community and Regional Planning, is now doing some teaching and is also, admirably, involved in a Committee studying the issue of workforce housing.

The high-rise mentality, directed by recent Vancouver Councils and implemented by Beasley is, in my view, actually divorced from a sense of place, and a sense of what the architecture is really creating in terms of social justice, and community.   After Beasley left the employ of the city of Vancouver, one of his largest projects was situated in Abu Dhabi in the United Arab Emirates, in charge of a new master plan, for what is probably the world's richest city - ruled by the whim of its royalty, under principles of gender inequality and lack of liberty that most Canadians would find abhorrent.   Foreign menial laborers, including what are essentially child slaves, are treated like medieval serfs, and abused without any recourse.   Foreign child slaves as young as four years old were until recently forced into positions as "camel jockeys", for the infamous camel races for the entertainment of the rich, because they were so light and their highly pitched screams were thought to spur on the camels.

The question, then, is does it matter if you are planning for a totalitarian state as opposed to a democratic state.   Should there be a different architecture in a free and liberal society that values social justice?   Should there be a different Planning for a society that recognizes and implements women's rights?   Shouldn't a Planning that is infused with Feminist sensibilities help to plan for affordable rental housing for the thousands of middle aged women who find themselves, upon divorce or death of a husband, thrust into the work force with no marketable skills except pouring coffee at minimum wage?   To me, a just urban planning in a liberal city in Canada must take into account the need to help such single women live a dignified life.   Shouldn't planning take into account family structures?   For example, in Vancouver we have many new immigrants from countries where extended families like to live together, to assist in the care of the elderly and the young.   The Vancouver Model of one and two bedrooms in high rises does not assist those who would like to maintain this lifestyle.

It seems to me, then that too few seem to realize that planning should not be merely some *technical* issue of zoning regulations and layout of streets and parks.   Planning by its very nature, involves a manifestation of cultural values.   It is these cultural values that our elected councilors should be directing their planning staff to implement in their technical plans.   Environmental sensibilities are one cultural value of Lotus Land, and esthetics are another.   It is time for Planners and Architects to move to the forefront of discussing how their talents can be utilized to further other cultural values and seek explicit directions from Municipal Councils regarding the values that are to be embraced.

If Vancouver wants to create zones of use dependant on family size, age, income, or any other criteria, then that should be debated.   And if the citizens accept the need for high density based on population increase in an area of limited buildable land, and agree to create such high density zones, they must be linked by rapid transit, first and foremost.   So much is said about developers in the Vancouver Model providing amenities, but the most important amenity to many people is the ability to get somewhere else in a reasonable amount of time.

Larry Beasley's concept plan for Abu Dhabi shows a series of dense neighbourhoods, each with a mosque in the middle.   That in itself shows how far Abu Dhabi is from Vancouver.   The community of worshippers has no parallel in Vancouver;   the architecture of a religious institution is totally *inclusive* for its adherents, but our architecture is totally *exclusive*, hoping that the community governed by the strata board of directors will compensate for lost neighbourhoods.

Dense neighbourhoods with congested streets may be good for the healthy folks between 20 and 70, but are they as good for the very young and the very old?

The architecture of *density* should be able to include *diversity*, and the architecture of rich *compensation* should be able to include *compassion*. The architecture of social *exclusivity* should be able to include social *inclusivity* and ultimately social justice.

As the McGill professor stated, there is a need for "place-making". Density is not in itself place-making. We must go beyond density to see what places we are really making, and stop patting ourselves on the back long enough to contemplate what are the proper ingredients for a place that is good for all our citizens. What kind of place ignores the real needs of young families and immigrants to find affordable housing somewhere near where they work?

If one wants to see a wonderful counterpoint to the Downtown condo towers, just stroll the street of the old Strathcona neighbourhood, just east of Chinatown. There one can see wonderful medium density row houses, duplexes and triplexes, as well as a mix of medium density social housing and retirement housing, old brick schoolhouses like Strathcona and Seymour Schools, and small parks with children playing. But what you will also see in this modest neighbourhood only blocks from the Downtown Eastside is pride of ownership, small lots lovingly cultivated, community gardens for those with little or no land, and a mix of new housing made to fit in to the historic streetscapes. Much of the work done to enhance and preserve such neighbourhoods was done when the City still had 'area" planners, that is, planners who were responsible for certain neighbourhoods, and therefore brought to the table a commitment to, and a knowledge of, the neighbourhood.

179

And surely, we should stop the silly accolades for architects who participated in the travesty of the leaky condos.   I shake my head when such architects bandy about the word "sustainability" when many of their previous buildings were so badly designed (for example without overhangs, without ways for water to escape between interior and exterior building walls, or were based on designs and materials used in near-desert conditions of California).   The most elementary form of sustainability is for the purchasers of the condos to have the peace of mind that the building will last for more than 10 years without major leakage problems or other major structural repairs.

One need only to go on the web, and read the horror stories featured in such sites as www.myleakycondo.com or www.bccondos.ca to understand the vastness of the problem with Vancouver condo buildings and how the mainstream media has been complicit with big developers to bamboozle people into buying units in poorly constructed buildings, designed and built by people who should have been drummed out of the industry years ago.

By creating the hype about property values and the desirability of living in a densified collection of poorly built condo towers, Vancouverism has again benefited the elites and hurt the large numbers of good faith buyers who will see the property values of their condo units decline.   The speculators and investors will all have "turned over" their units and made their profits, leaving the inevitable repair bills for leakage problems to the people who can least afford to come up with the money for these unexpected expenses.

The basic point is that the Vancouver skyline only looks good from a distance.   A closer inspection will reveal that Vancouver has the most flawed housing stock in Canada.

Alas, the Lotus Land of the Sky, exists only for the developers, contractors, architects, engineers, and realtors getting rich from the "Vancouver Model"; by the time real purchasers seek to inhabit that land, the lotuses all have been eaten, and the "mariners" have moved on.

Chapter 15

A Pause to Look at Some Numbers and the Economic Forecast

"While the individual man is an insoluble puzzle, in the aggregate he becomes a mathematical certainty. You can, for example, never foretell what any one man will be up to, but you can say with precision what an average number will be up to. Individuals vary, but percentages remain constant. So says the statistician."

~Arthur Conan Doyle

Before we discuss the issue of whether Vancouver is transitioning from a normal city to a high end "resort", let us review some statistical data, to better understand how Vancouver is continuing to grow.

According to CBC News, the number of Canadians aged 55 to 64 — those most likely to be thinking about retirement — jumped by 28 per cent in the past five years to 3.7 million.

Baby boomers, (born between 1946 and 1964) account for close to one-third of the country's 32 million people. According to *Medical News Today*, the number of baby boomers turning 60 in Canada is growing at a rate of over 1,000 per day. The life expectancy for a 60 year old in Canada is over 20 years. And, according to Robert L. Brown, in his study called "Future Age of Retirement" in the *Canadian Investment Review,* Fall 2002, the average age of retirement for Canadians in the next 40 years will fluctuate between 60 and 61.

Accordingly, we have some thousand or more people in Canada retiring every day, with a future life expectancy of twenty years.

In a 2006 study by Harris Interactive for the HSBC Banking Group, for Canadian respondents, 24 per cent indicated they wanted to work into retirement for the money, while 23 per cent wanted something meaningful to do, 21 per cent to keep physically active, 18 per cent for mental stimulation, 11 per cent to connect with others. Of the Canadians polled, fifty-eight per cent perceived retirement as an opportunity for a whole new chapter in life, while 22 per cent saw it as a time of rest, 15 per cent as the continuation of what life was, and 4 per cent as the beginning of the end.

So, it seems that we shall have large groups of Canadians retiring, some wanting to work for the money, but even more seeking something meaningful to do and to keep active, with a majority of Canadians viewing retirement as an opportunity for a new chapter in life.

With the high costs of health insurance in the United States, and the uninsurability of those with recent major health problems like cancer or heart disease, the idea of retiring to Florida or Arizona will become problematic.

With the above figures, it is reasonable to suggest, that many Canadians, will be seeking the climate and lifestyle of Vancouver and other areas of British Columbia. Moreover, in seeking something meaningful to do and seeking mental stimulation, they will as likely be wanting to move to large cities as to rural areas or golf resorts. For those baby boomers who have grown used to the cultural amenities, sporting events, state of the art medical care, and other opportunities found only in large cities, Vancouver may well be the retirement destination of choice.

It seems obvious that the Provincial government's policy priorities have only exacerbated the high cost of housing, and therefore seek to favour high end housing, including retirement housing, over housing for young working families. When the Provincial government opted to support the 2010 Winter Olympics and a massive new convention centre for Vancouver, that was bound to have effects in the construction sector. These decisions were made in one of the hottest housing markets in Vancouver's history, where the number of private sector developments were straining the supplies of labour and materials, and creating price inflation in construction, which of course is reflected in higher housing costs.

The decision by the Province to add the venues of the 2010 Olympics and to build the new convention centre were like pouring oil into the fire of construction costs and accordingly housing costs. The data is now coming in.

In an article in the November 20, 2007 *Vancouver Sun,* citing Statistics Canada figures, it was reported that the cost of apartment-building construction in Metro Vancouver rose almost 14% over the last 12 months, far ahead of the national rate. (Toronto's rate only went up 5%, despite a condo construction boom in that city.) With these figures, one can question the merit of a policy of creating huge demand for non-residential construction in a time when residential construction costs are reaching a crisis.

As we shall discuss, in the next chapter, the "resortification" of Vancouver is being attained to the benefit of those in the hospitality and construction sectors, and to the detriment of average working people, whose government sector has made the choices that have resulted in the rise of costs for new apartment buildings.

Moreover, in a recent report by Vancouver commercial realtor, David Goodman (cited in the aforementioned *Vancouver Sun* article), the sale price per unit in apartment buildings being sold is now up to $184,000 in Vancouver city and $118,000 in Greater Vancouver. In popular areas like Kitsilano the increase was even more, being more than 35%, up to $236,000 per rental unit. With a vacancy rate of less than 1%, and no policies in existence in British Columbia or Vancouver to give inducements to private sector developers to construct new rental units to increase the supply, there is little wonder that the prices are escalating wildly.

And still the government of B.C. boasts of its program to provide income supplements to renters of modest income, which increases the demand without increasing the supply. With money to help the hospitality industry and the construction industry, and no money to give as inducements to create moderate priced rental housing, the governments in Lotus Land have made their choice. Now the data is clear, as to the effects of that choice.

Now let us turn to the issue of immigration to Vancouver, and future population growth. What about continued Chinese immigration? Figures from BC Stats show that in 2005, the Vancouver area received 12,939 immigrants from the Peoples' Republic of China, 2118 from Taiwan, and 631 from Hong Kong. For the Chinese from the PRC, this was an increase of about 2500 from 2004, which 2004 figure was in turn an increase of about 1000 from 2003.

British Columbia as a whole receives about one third of all immigrants from the PRC to Canada, and over 70% of the total to Canada from Taiwan, and about 38% of those from Hong Kong.

Currently, the largest group of business immigrants are those from China. China remains just ahead of India as the largest source of total immigrants. When it comes to Chinese immigrants, 2005 figures show that 57.5% are skilled workers, 13.4% are business immigrants, and 21.6% are family of existing residents.

It is fair to conclude that there is at this time, no let up of skilled workers and wealthier business immigrants from China to Vancouver. The Chinese continue to create population growth in Vancouver, and they continue to have among their immigrants many who are in a position to buy properties in Vancouver either immediately upon entry or a few years down the road.

In any event, we know that Greater Vancouver experienced a population growth of nearly 60%, from 1.2 million people in 1981 to 1.98 million in 2001. According to the Metro Vancouver website, the population for Greater Vancouver increased 6.5% from 2001 to 2006, increasing from 1.98 million to almost 2.12 million. Similar rates of growth are expected for the future. The Greater Vancouver Regional District (now Metro Vancouver) expects a total population of 2.6 million by 2021 and nearly 3 million by 2031 . The Design Centre for Sustainability at the University of British Columbia, at a 2006 program, assumed a total regional population of four million in 50 years, by 2056.

In a Canada Mortgage and Housing Corporation forecast released in November 2007, it was projected a yearly increase in new residents of 35,000 to Greater Vancouver and an increase of jobs by 33,000. With such increases in population and job growth, CMHC projected that the average single-family home in Greater Vancouver would rise to $900,000. It seems clear that the average in Vancouver proper would be over $1 million.

And despite the myth that not so many people work downtown anymore, thus obviating the need for either expressways or high-speed public transit, the Fraser Valley Real Estate Board came up with some interesting statistics published on November 6, 2007 in *The Vancouver Sun:* the District of Mission, with its population of about 35,000, some 70 kilometres east of Vancouver, and the eastern terminus of the West Coast Express commuter rail service, between Mission and downtown Vancouver, had the greatest one year price increases for single family homes within that Board's Fraser Valley region.
While Surrey's increase was 8.4%, Langley's was 9.5%, and Abbotsford's was 10.3%, the District of Mission's was 18.4%! It seems that with the right rapid commuter rail service, the suburban areas of Vancouver will boom, leading to higher population and higher real estate values.

One can argue that the boom has already started. One developer of condos in Pitt Meadows advertises in its marketing a study showing projected real estate price increases for the next year there of over 10%. Perhaps the beginnings of a recession in late 2008 will reduce that estimate; but as long as new residents move to Greater Vancouver, demand will keep prices higher than elsewhere.

In Surrey, the Cental City condo towers of 36 and 40 floors are said to have sold out 900 homes in the first thirty hours after the sales office opened.

What proportion of these condos in Greater Vancouver, that seem to be snapped up within a day of availability, and which will not be ready for occupancy for a couple of years, are in fact being sold to those who will occupy them, and what percentage to investors or speculators? (Investors being those who will rent them out as investments, and speculators being those who intend to "flip" them in a year or two as the condos near completion.)

From the number of advertisements in the real estate section advertising "Assignments", one can conclude that a sizeable number of units are going to speculators. From the fact that almost no purpose-built apartment buildings are built in Greater Vancouver, one may conclude that there is a whole marketplace of investors buying condo units to rent to tenants, who have a good income to pay high rent, but do not have the savings to put down towards purchase.

In a *Vancouver Sun* real estate section article on November 10, 2007, Diane Delves, president of Quantum Properites, says of her 188 unit Tamarind project in Abbotsford (one hour from Vancouver) that she expects 40% of buyers to be investors. No wonder, when the price per square foot in Abbotsford in her project is running at less than $400 per square foot ($279,000 for 746 square feet) compared to over $750 per square foot in Vancouver. The suburban towns like Abbotsford are becoming the new Vancouver for young families and middle class people of all ages, as Vancouver becomes the preserve of the wealthy. Abbotsford now has a population of 140,000 people and a good airport.

Just look at the statistics: A recent Statistics Canada study, quoted in a story in the November 10, 2007 issue of the *Vancouver Sun*, states that only half of those between the age of 25 and 39 own any type of home in Vancouver, compared with 71% of Canadians living in rural communities. The same article stated that it is not surprising that buyers are moving to the Fraser Valley, where the average detached home is expected to sell for $250,000 less than in Greater Vancouver, according to the B.C. Real Estate Association's Fall 2007 Housing Forecast.

It is inevitable that the future will bring the completion of more rapid transit lines, thus integrating further the City of Vancouver with the rest of the Fraser Valley region.   This integration is bound to affect the cultural foundations of Vancouver, just the same as the growth of the "905" suburbs in Toronto, have changed the make-up of the Toronto area and its culture.

Now, what of the economic mix of companies that do business in Vancouver?   What areas are growing the fastest, and what does that tell us about Vancouver's population mix and housing needs for the future?

It is clear that the last decade in Vancouver witnessed a diversified group of forestry, energy, biotech, communications, and consumer/retail companies.   It is as yet unclear whether the Canadian dollar will maintain its strength (as of late 2007) against the American dollar, and what the effect of that will be on such economic sectors as film-making, forestry, high end real estate, and others.

It is possible to get some good data about British Columbia's publicly traded companies. The *Vancouver Sun,* in conjunction with the Sauder School of Business at University of British Columbia and Ernst & Young LLP. has published a list of the 50 fastest-growing public companies in B.C. and the 50 strongest companies in B.C.   (The companies are deemed to be B.C. companies if their headquarters are in B.C. and/or a significant proportion of business activities are located in the province.

The 2007 study shows that the mining sector constituted 31 of the fasted growing companies in B.C., and mining constituted 29 of the strongest companies.   These miners were digging up gold, silver and even tungsten in places like Ghana, China and Peru.   So, what Vancouver has is the wealthy executives and investors in these profitable and fast-growing companies.   The miners live somewhere else, often in another country, but the money people, the high paid executives live in Vancouver.

Mining is but one example of a variety of businesses run around the world by people living in wealth and tranquility in Lotus Land. From Chinese industrialists, to international real estate developers to a plethora of internet businesses and computer related industries, Vancouver gets the top earners, and the underlings work and live elsewhere. As noted earlier we also have an undue share of white collar criminals.

On my monthly flights to Ontario, I am always amazed at the Vancouver residents I meet on the plane or in the airport who are deriving the income used in Vancouver from enterprises in other parts of Canada, and around the world.

But what is so obviously missing in Vancouver is a healthy, diverse, and growing corporate sector. Vancouver is the only one of Canada's six largest cities to lose head office jobs between 1999 and 2005. Head office jobs here declined by an amazing 30 percent. In our concluding chapter, we shall look at the consequences of being a resort, rather than a business oriented city.

In addition to the fast growing mining industry in the sector of public companies, we have a lot of our economic output in Vancouver centred around real estate and construction. Jock Finlayson, the executive vice-president of the Business Council of British Columbia, in a piece in *The Vancouver Sun*, on November 26, 2007, argues that an economic boom tied to the construction sector cannot go on forever and that we need more globally competitive export industries. He quotes his organization's own study that seven of the ten fastest-growing industries in B.C. are "part of or closely tied to the broad construction sector." Mr. Finlayson seeks to distinguish between those industries satisfying a local demand, like real estate and construction, retail and other consumer services and much of the public sector, with those industries which export. These industries, which have lately been hit hard by the high Canadian dollar, would include forestry, oil and gas, and coal, as well as tourism, film production, call centres, greenhouse growers, and parts of the high-tech sector.

But as long as Greater Vancouver continues to attract immigration, from both the rest of Canada and offshore, then the real estate and construction sector may well continue to boom - unless of course economic conditions become such as to cause extremely high interest rates, or a serious recession, or world events and wars are such as to bring economic dislocation.

And unless one believes the arguments of the great American urban critic James Howard Kunstler, in his book, *The Long Emergency*. Kuntsler argues that we have now started a long, precipitous decline due to an inevitable future shortage of oil and other petro-chemical products, which will cause massive dislocation to our present oil-dependent economies. He argues that an auto and trucking-dependent economy will inevitable flounder as present net exporters of oil deplete their supplies and become net importers of oil, or at least stop exporting.

Kunstler believes that the U.S. and other western countries falsely believe that technological advances in alternate fuels will save us from a long decline leading to a fundamental reorganization of commercial and residential life to accord with the new realities. Whatever is the case with Canada's own resources, a serious decline in the American economy will of course drag down Canada with it.

In a recent email exchange, Kunstler told me: "I would be serenely confident that real estate prices in Vancouver will spiral down sooner or later." But then he added: "Unless the supply of foreign money and drug money is absolutely inexhaustible."

Whether Kunstler is right or not, we can say *at present* Vancouver serves as the idyllic and beautiful locale for homes of leading executives, entrepreneurs, and criminals, as well as the part time home for wealthy individuals from actors to successful writers and artists, and to international businessmen looking for a stable resort-like environment in this age of globalization. In the next chapter, we attempt some conclusions.

However, hanging over Vancouver's "success story", like a black cloud threatening rain, is the effect of the U.S. financial "meltdown", and the concern of what it will do to Canada in general, and Vancouver, in particular.

We can suggest that the mariners of Lotus Land are first and foremost connoisseurs of fine lotus leaves and consumers of things beautiful. In this, they are poorly equipped to adapt to recessionary economies where, firstly, harvesting the assets comes to an end because there is no more credit available to finance the endless harvest, and, secondly, there are not enough customers left with sufficient money to buy the harvest.

I am finishing this book just as the late September 2008 financial "earthquake" has struck the United States, with its after shocks around the world. Starting with predatory mortgage lending practices, leading to mammoth defaults and repossessions, proceeding through the effects on the credit granting institutions that purchased packages of insecure investments, and to the insolvency of investment bankers, hedge fund dealers, and major banks, all leading to a crisis in the stock markets where huge values of stocks were lost in a week's time, the American economy has some major issues, even with the $700-billion "bailout" by the Government.

We could be seeing the end of the era of great consumption by the middle classes who have been living like the upper classes (due to mortgaging their appreciating real estate and using credit cards like the mariners of Lotos Land used lotos leaves). To those heirs of the Lotos Eaters who are experts in nothing so much as consumption of material goods and enjoyment of the esthetic, this may appear to be the end of the world as they know it.

To the media, whose newspapers, devoted whole sections to Homes, Travel, and Autos, and hence minimized the truly important issues of our time in favour of the encouragement of consumption and consumer*ism*, you have been part of the problem.

As is discussed in the next and concluding chapter, the municipal politicians, embracing Vancouverism, have helped turn Vancouver into a Resort. Will these politicians now be accountable when economic conditions world-wide mean there will be fewer tourists and wealthy buyers interested in what Vancouver the Resort is now offering?

I suggest that it will soon become apparent that the years 2000 to 2008 were among the best years in history for Vancouver's economy. Vancouver, like most other places, will have to struggle with the effects of a deep recession for the next few years. Accordingly, there will be a realization that Vancouver used up some of its best years in boasting about itself, creating big shows like the Olympics and the Convention Centre, and, with the exception of the province buying up some SRO hotels, all but ignored affordable housing for low and middle income workers, in particular the need for rental housing and "off-market" workforce owned units.

How will Vancouver cope when recessionary times kill the demand for the tourism, high-end housing, and investment scams upon which it has relied for the last half-dozen years?

The problem discussed in Chapter 2 is Vancouver's unwillingness to look and learn from events happening beyond its borders. California would be the state in the United States which is most similar in its Lotus attitudes to British Columbia. Although the situation with subprime mortgages in California is very different with the situation in Vancouver, it is interesting to note how Californians have dealt with the effects of mortgage foreclosures within the middle class in California. One of the most tragic things is that news stories have shown that many of the people losing their homes are in almost a state of denial right up to the end. When the end comes, many simply walk away from houses full of furniture, large-screen TVs and the like, and there have even been reports of family pets abandoned as their owners rush to vacate their houses.

It seems that the skill-set developed by the middle class in American Lotus Land, the ability to be aggressive consumers of housing, credit, electronic toys and autos, is of little use when it comes to the skills needed to deal with recessionary times. Will Vancouverites show the same sense of denial and lack of planning?

It seems that the Mariners of Lotos Land prefer to stay stoned on the lotos leaves and consume the harvests of Lotos Land, rather than deal with the challenges of scarcity and the need for planning. In a deep recession, the governed and the governors have to make hard decisions. Hard decisions need to be based on some understanding of Good and Evil, so as to assess priorities. But if the lotos eaters have based their whole lives on negating the idea of Good versus Evil, and living as if endless consumption was a possibility in this world, they are ill-equipped for the recession that is upon us.

As is discussed in the next and concluding chapter, the municipal politicians, embracing Vancouverism, have helped turn Vancouver into a Resort. The narcissistic ideology of viewing British Columbia as the "Best Place on Earth" intrinsically minimizes the problems of those who are left wanting in paradise. We must ask what will happen to the Lotos Eaters when economic conditions world-wide mean there will be fewer tourists and wealthy buyers interested in what Vancouver the Resort is now offering. What will happen when there is no longer an appreciation of housing prices to support property flipping and abuse of credit? Will Vancouverism adapt or will it implode?

Chapter 16: Conclusion

Money and the Moderate Climate – the Resortification of Vancouver

"I summer in the HAMPTONS…
I winter in ASPEN…
My home – THE RITZ-CARLTON, VANCOUVER"

- advertisement for the new Residences of the Ritz-Carleton, Vancouver, being floors 27 to 60 above the 26 floors of the future hotel, with residences ranging in cost from $2.25 million to $29 million.

Letter to the Editor by Vancouverite Barry Shanko in the October 26, 2007 edition of *The Vancouver Sun:*
"On the Oct. 24 front page: 'Vancouver condo sells for record $18 million.'
On the Oct. 24 front page of (*The Vancouver Sun's) Westcoast News* (section):
'Looking for a place to live.'
Does this say that this city has its priorities wrong, wrong, wrong and it's about time the citizens rose up and said to heck with business, international investors, upscale yuppies and all the others who are turning this region into an 'only rich folks wanted' city?"

"Big money goes around the world
Big money give and take
Big money done a power of good
Big money make mistakes
Big money got a heavy hand
Big money take control
Big money got a mean streak
Big money got no soul…"

-Neil Peart and Rush, "The Big Money" from the album, *Power Windows, 1985*

We conclude this exploration of the political culture of Vancouverism. Although the last chapter took a brief look at some statistics, we have made a very *subjective* journey through Canada's Lotus Land.

By going back to Tennyson's "The Lotos-Eaters", I hope that the ideological themes of Lotus Land have been a useful analytic tool to understanding Vancouver's political culture. For every culture is a reflection of the preponderant "state of mind" of various key groups. No culture in the West, where freedom reigns, can be monolithic. But certain themes must be identified, and these themes are necessarily subjective. We hope that the inquiry that we have started will stimulate more debate about the foundational values both here in Vancouver and elsewhere.

When all is said and done, Vancouver's political culture comes down to three things – money, the moderate climate, and the legacy of the Lotos.

And when money and a moderate climate prevail in a place, that place is likely to become, not so much a regular city, but a *resort,* especially when the legacy of the Lotos, stresses pleasure and calm, rather than industriousness and social justice. It is my conclusion, that by emphasizing high end housing, a billion dollar new convention centre (at time of writing projected to be 80% over budget), recreational opportunities, and the 2010 Winter Olympics, Vancouver's politicians have been participating in the *resortification* of Vancouver.

Trevor Boddy, in the *Vancouver* magazine article of April, 2007, explores the nature of a resort that has turned away from corporate growth:

"We're settling into a Rio-like future as a resort attached to our festering favela, the Downtown Eastside. Vancouver is a wonderful place to visit, to play, to shoot up, to check out of a career, to retire, but it's no longer a serious business centre. The first people I heard describe Vancouver as a "resort" were Hong Kong- and Taiwan-born businessmen as they re-aligned their investments towards China after

194

briefly nesting here in the 1990s. The resortification of our downtown has been a quiet secret in Vancouver's development and urban planning communities for a decade; real estate brokers long ago stopped listing land here as potential office sites—the returns from condos being so much higher. Only recently has the nine-to-one ratio of condo-to-office tower construction since 2000 on our land-limited downtown peninsula become a public issue."

But living in a resort means the adoption of a whole different set of priorities for a municipality.   For example, the hospitality sector assumes key importance, and local politicians must give more perks to that sector than the average citizens who happen to be working in some other sector, and don't benefit directly from hotel and restaurant revenue.

The best example is the expenditure by the province and the municipality of nearly a billion dollars on a new convention centre. The other is the huge expenditures for a short term event like the Olympics. There is an unease in Vancouver, not entirely articulated yet, that there is something of a perversion of priorities in Lotus Land.

There are other more subtle costs to living in a resort.   Vancouver is now home to five high end hotels that have pricy condos in the upper floors over the hotel. The new Ritz-Carlton hotel and condo project at 1151 West Georgia will have 123 residences in the upper floors. But not everyone understands the financial imperative for the developers in creating these mega-priced residences under the cachet of the Ritz-Carlton name, with the amenities of a fine hotel.   In a *Vancouver Sun* article on November 10, 2007, condo marketing guru Bob Rennie explains:

"You will not see a five-star hotel built in North America without condos above it. The cost of providing the services and the security and building out those rooms, given today's room rates, is not sustainable for the hotel. So they build the condos and they take the profit from the condos to buy down the hotel, so that they can have a sustainable five-star climate. It's just a fact."

As reported by the *Globe and Mail*'s British Columbia columnist Gary Mason on May 17, 2008, Rennie has sold 60 per cent of the 123 residences at the Ritz-Carlton, scheduled to be completed in three years, at an average of **$2300. per square foot!** Accordingly, the rich Chinese, Koreans, Iranians and Russians, who are buying these units, feel they are a good place to park their money, and are happy to pay $2.3 million for a 1000 square foot condo that will not even be ready for three years.

So, high-priced housing is helping to subsidize the cost of high-priced hotels. To my mind, high-priced housing should also help to subsidize the cost of low-priced housing; but the needs of those in the resort-industry are, apparently, paramount.

Another fact in a resort, is that your transportation links to the airport take priority over your transportation links for your workers. Accordingly, we understand why the Canada Line rapid transit line to the airport took priority, in the eyes of local Vancouver politicians, to the needs of workers living in the Fraser Valley to get into Vancouver with the speed and convenience of rapid transit. We may not like it, but understanding that Vancouver is transforming itself into a resort at least makes clear the actions being undertaken at City Council and elsewhere.

Frankly, resortification carries other effects, not all positive. When resorts cater to *pleasure*, they attract the full range of sexual services and various forms of prostitution. Prostitution, like other illegal businesses attract organized crime, violent turf battles, and illegal immigrants. These illegal sex workers are recruited into the semi-slavery of prostitution, where most of their fees go to the "handlers" who have to be paid back for bringing them to the country, housing and feeding them, and providing drugs, so that the prostitute herself ends up with negligible income - and being illegal, has no recourse to get out of her terrible situation. In any resort featuring prostitution, the apparently glamorous surface hides a seedy and disgusting underground that debases any city that seeks out such resort status.

The idea of a "resort" may conjure up the idyllic life on the beaches of lotus land, with ski trips to nearby Whistler, but the reality is as much that of prostitution, gambling, excessive drinking, and drugs. When the resort has a lot of rainy weather (actually, on average, there is measurable precipitation on 166 days per year and some measurable sun on 289 days), and the tourist is not skiing at Whistler, what is going on indoors? *The Georgia Straight* newspaper, a popular tabloid, carries some five or six pages of classified ads with pictures for prostitutes and massage parlours.

Who, then, gets to decide what type of resort Vancouver will be? Will it be an Orlando, with theme parks, or will be it a Las Vegas ("what happens in Vegas, stays in Vegas"), or even a Bangkok, full of sex tourists?   Might it partner with Victoria as a destination for "seniors' tourism"? Is it to be the main destination for gay tourism? Or is it a type of resort for international wealthy businessmen who keep a home here as a precaution against political and social instability in their home countries? Urban planning should be preoccupied with whether Vancouver wants to become a resort, and, if so, what kind of resort.

Arguably the narcissistic talk of Vancouver being the "best", most livable", or whatever, is meant to "rally the troops", that is, the citizens of Vancouver, into supporting policies that seem not to be in the interest of the average working person. Instead, these are policies in the interests of the hospitality sector, the real estate and construction sector, and numerous city planners and architects, who, concentrating on mega-projects and high-end buildings, can assume a rock-star like status.

While the celebrities in a city like Seattle include numerous business innovators like the founders of Microsoft and Starbucks, in Vancouver business celebrities are more likely to include top real estate developers and real estate agents, mining and forestry executives and their brokers and promoters, plus high-end restaurant owners, and their big-name executive chefs.

Not that there is anything terribly wrong with a vibrant hospitality sector - as long as local government and other elites are honest about what they are doing, and the choices being made are clearly articulated and weighed for the general good, not just a few groups.

Perhaps recognition that we are becoming a "resort" is a first step towards housing the employees of the resort.   For the beautiful ski resort of Whistler years ago realized that it must take steps to house its workers, and has now implemented a variety of affordable housing programs including owned housing with covenants for restrictions on sale price, so as to keep the units affordable for future workers.

Are there any reasons for optimism?   To be sure, there are many good people in Vancouver who, when given the understanding that there *are* policies and programs available, will certainly start to advocate for them.   For example, SmartGrowth B.C. has now shown that we can overcome the "Anti-comparisonism" described in our Emperor's New City of Chapter 2.   Two new excellent surveys of programs in other provinces and states of the U.S. can be found at:

> Review of Best Practices in Affordable Housing at
> http://www.smartgrowth.bc.ca/Portals/0/Downloads/SGBC_Affordabl
> e_Housing_Report_2007.pdf

> Affordable Housing: A Smart Growth Toolkit for BC Municipalities
> http://www.smartgrowth.bc.ca/Portals/0/Downloads/SGBC_Affordabl
> e_Housing_Toolkit.pdf

And it is a hopeful sign that the 2008 EcoDensity policy of Mayor Sullivan has been sent back to staff for further work, as it obviously did not address the real problems of affordable housing.

In addition, people are starting to protest: In early 2008, grass roots protests started with residents of the 224-unit Little Mountain social housing complex in Vancouver, who were being urged to move to make way for a new, more upscale, mixed housing development. Then by March, 2008, demonstrations grew to 15 "stands" on street corners. The stands are silent vigils designed to attract awareness to the problems of both lack of affordable rental housing and rising homelessness.   By April, there were a total of 40 stands in Greater

Vancouver and dozens more in other communities across British Columbia. These stands are one-hour silent protests, with the protesters generally wearing identical tourquoise-blue scarves on street corners on Saturdays. The stands are now being organized by Church groups, groups for action on mental health, and youth groups.

Accordingly, if there will be progress on affordable housing, it will come from pressure from the bottom up. The elites and politicians have shown a failure to adequately deal with the problem. Hopefully peaceful street demonstrations will sway enough citizens of Vancouver to demand that the politicians take action.

But, a culture of promoting social justice has not yet overcome a culture designed to promote quick and easy money. A culture of "scamming" draws those new immigrants who are interested in also being scammers or criminals. Vancouver's history of tolerance for stock fraud, white collar crime and inability to put gang leaders and their minions in jail, effectively draws more of the same, confident that this resort, similar to Miami Beach and Las Vegas, is the best place to do business. The resortification is just part of the picture. Money, the moderate climate and the legacy of the logos are the foundations of the political culture, to be sure. But the walls holding up the structure are the flagrant disregard for working people, honest small businessman, honest investors, and others who are so often the losers in a culture that does not care to prosecute, and does not even care to *denounce* crooked stock promoters, predatory environmentalist teachers, or builder-developers ripping off purchasers with leaky condos.

When one begins to understand this, certain parallels become apparent. For example, Vancouver has been building a new rapid transit line from Downtown to the Airport in Richmond, along Cambie Street, which is a fairly well developed shopping street, of primarily small independent businesses. When proposals to build the SkyTrain Canada Line along Cambie Street first emerged, they were heavily protested by residents and business owners who argued in favour of using an existing, but out-of-use Arbutus Street rail corridor instead. (However, such an argument was doomed in the face of the political power of the upper income residential neighbours with multi-million dollar homes near the Arbutus rail corridor.)

Once the decision was made to use the Cambie alignment for the Canada Line anyway, residents along the corridor successfully persuaded authorities to put the rail line in a tunnel instead of running it as a surface route. Nonetheless, to save money the Canada Line switched from a tunnel to a more time-consuming cut-and-cover method which has introduced much disruption to traffic and business along the corridor during the construction. As such, even though it costs less than using a tunnel boring machine, the project has destroyed some small businesses, forced others to move, and cost most hundreds of thousands of dollar in lost business, because, for an inordinate amount of time, there is the equivalent of a two-storey hole running down the middle of the street. Where previously there were 3 lanes of traffic going in each direction, there have been, during the construction, only 1 lane each way, with substantial closing off of side street access to Cambie Street, which discourages those shoppers who would arrive by automobile.

This business interruption has lasted for two years. While the small businesses are of course protesting their fate, the actual landowners have been quiet, because they know that once the line is finished, their properties will be worth much more, as the transit line will bring with it, increased densities and re-development. So we have a case of a public benefit being created on the backs of, and to the detriment of, small businesses. Some two years into the construction, there is still no government program of compensation.

There is a pattern here, and not a very nice one. The Canada Line to the airport will help the resort of Downtown Vancouver, and the high income people who routinely use the airport. There is a complete disregard for those who are the "losers" in the project. These small businessmen, already paying property tax at five to six times the residential rate (which is much higher than most places in Canada) are also being asked to shoulder a disproportionate share of the economic cost of building this rapid transit.

Likewise, the thousands of investors in sham stock and investment frauds based in Vancouver, are generally without recourse, while many of the promoters, financiers, "executives" and their facilitators in the legal and accounting community have not only profited handsomely, but still have their reputations intact. One of the most flagrant of the financiers, who has received numerous honours for his community work, is routinely described in the fawning press as "colourful", a "stellar player" of the VSE in the '70s, and such similar accolades that hide the shambles that was created by an out-of-control, substantially unregulated investment community.

Likewise there are the thousands of "losers" in the condo game, who bought leaky condos, sometimes from some of the biggest names in Vancouver condo development and construction, who continue to do business, make their millions, and continue to be spoken of reverentially in the local society pages (see especially the sycophantic pieces by Malcolm Parry in both *The Vancouver Sun* and *Vancouver* magazine) and some of the business pages (with the notable exception of David Baines in the *Sun*, who, almost single-handedly, acts as a light shining on the unscrupulous underpinnings of the Vancouver investment community).

Vancouver is infamous for its historical booms and busts, especially in the real estate market. Notwithstanding the huge inflations of the years 2000 to 2008, is there anyone who has observed the construction business for the last thirty years, who believes all the hype about continued buying of high priced product being the best investment an individual can make? Moreover, everyone knows that a good percentage of the downtown condos appear to be unlived in. The prevailing view is that these are somehow owned by wealthy offshore businessmen or corporations who hold them for the few weeks a year that the businessmen are in Vancouver to do business. Doubtless, some of them are owned for that purpose. Some also may be owned by businessmen in countries that are not democracies, and who want to have a residence in a more stable country, if they quickly need one. But does anyone truly believe that these reasons alone account for the thousands of apparently unused units?

Without a very difficult investigation, the answer cannot be clear. However, we suggest that many of the units are part of a sophisticated money-laundering operation, whereby the "dirty" proceeds of the massive drug trade, and other illegal activities, can be placed in a Canadian "growth" asset. A few years later, the units are sold, and then the money is "clean" proceeds of real estate.

So, wherever we look, Vancouver's masses are inevitably used in the service of a corrupted system that promotes criminality more than integrity, and promotes profit for the few over social justice for the many.

James Howard Kunstler, about whom I wrote in the last chapter, spoke at Simon Fraser University in Vancouver in late January, 2008. One of his interesting points is that, sometimes what he terms "group psychology" causes people to do, or not to do, certain things. He used as an example, the problem of the sub-prime loans in the United States, that so hurt the housing market and the whole economy. Kunstler stated that for some reason, "bankers forgot that you should not lend money to people who have no prospect of paying it back."

And after studying the tremendous growth rate of Las Vegas, and casinos everywhere, Kunstler concludes that America's fastest growing religion is the "worship of unearned riches", based on the theological position that "it is possible to get something for nothing."

Irrational exuberance, then, causes some odd choices. Vancouver has a few casinos, but nothing out of the ordinary compared to most places across the country. However, one might conclude the religion of unearned riches, based on getting something for nothing, in Vancouver, manifests itself through excessive (and unearned?) real estate gains, white collar crime, fast and easy drug money, and the like. To this extent, Vancouver is on no higher a moral plane than Las Vegas.

If Vancouver is still predominantly a Lotus Land, can this Lotus Land be overlaid with policies that create, in addition to pleasure, a social justice? Can a Lotus Land co-exist with policies to create a livable city for ALL of its citizens, throughout ALL of its suburbs, not just those who "got in early" or those who are very rich? Can housing be looked at as basic right for human dignity, not a romantic notion of real estate marketers?

Can the intellectuals of Vancouver begin to understand that progressivism is built on higher values than just tolerance? Can we lose tolerance for the underside of the Lotos, and begin to create a richer more values-based culture - one that acknowledges that all of us have a responsibility to each other, including the young and low income working people?

Can we move on from the Lotus values of *looking* good and *feeling* good to the higher value of *doing* good?

Can we appreciate Beauty, without *worshipping* it?

Can we reject the Lotos Eaters' abandonment of their children, and plan for the housing needs and the child care needed by the next generation?

Can the culture of *Vancouverism*, free itself of narcissism, tolerism, criminality, and greed, rise above its roots in both the Lotos and the Wild West, and *in reality*, become sustainable in its livability for all?

We certainly hope so.

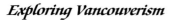

Appendix:

"The Lotos-Eaters" by Alfred Tennyson

"Courage!" he said, and pointed toward the land,
"This mounting wave will roll us shoreward soon."
In the afternoon they came unto a land
In which it seemed always afternoon.
All round the coast the languid air did swoon,
Breathing like one that hath a weary dream.
Full-faced above the valley stood the moon;
And like a downward smoke, the slender stream
Along the cliff to fall and pause and fall did seem.

A land of streams! some, like a downward smoke,
Slow-dropping veils of thinnest lawn, did go;
And some thro' wavering lights and shadows broke,
Rolling a slumbrous sheet of foam below.
They saw the gleaming river seaward flow
From the inner land: far off, three mountain-tops,
Three silent pinnacles of aged snow,
Stood sunset-flush'd: and, dew'd with showery drops,
Up-clomb the shadowy pine above the woven copse.

The charmed sunset linger'd low adown
In the red West: thro' mountain clefts the dale
Was seen far inland, and the yellow down
Border'd with palm, and many a winding vale
And meadow, set with slender galingale;
A land where all things always seem'd the same!
And round about the keel with faces pale,
Dark faces pale against that rosy flame,
The mild-eyed melancholy Lotos-eaters came.

Branches they bore of that enchanted stem,
Laden with flower and fruit, whereof they gave
To each, but whoso did receive of them,

And taste, to him the gushing of the wave
Far far away did seem to mourn and rave
On alien shores; and if his fellow spake,
His voice was thin, as voices from the grave;
And deep-asleep he seem'd, yet all awake,
And music in his ears his beating heart did make.

They sat them down upon the yellow sand,
Between the sun and moon upon the shore;
And sweet it was to dream of Fatherland,
Of child, and wife, and slave; but evermore
Most weary seem'd the sea, weary the oar,
Weary the wandering fields of barren foam.
Then some one said, "We will return no more";
And all at once they sang, "Our island home
Is far beyond the wave; we will no longer roam."

Choric Song

I

There is sweet music here that softer falls
Than petals from blown roses on the grass,
Or night-dews on still waters between walls
Of shadowy granite, in a gleaming pass;
Music that gentlier on the spirit lies,
Than tir'd eyelids upon tir'd eyes;
Music that brings sweet sleep down from the blissful skies.
Here are cool mosses deep,
And thro' the moss the ivies creep,
And in the stream the long-leaved flowers weep,
And from the craggy ledge the poppy hangs in sleep.

II

Why are we weigh'd upon with heaviness,
And utterly consumed with sharp distress,
While all things else have rest from weariness?
All things have rest: why should we toil alone,
We only toil, who are the first of things,
And make perpetual moan,
Still from one sorrow to another thrown:
Nor ever fold our wings,
And cease from wanderings,
Nor steep our brows in slumber's holy balm;
Nor harken what the inner spirit sings,
"There is no joy but calm!"
Why should we only toil, the roof and crown of things?

III

Lo! in the middle of the wood,
The folded leaf is woo'd from out the bud
With winds upon the branch, and there
Grows green and broad, and takes no care,
Sun-steep'd at noon, and in the moon
Nightly dew-fed; and turning yellow
Falls, and floats adown the air.
Lo! sweeten'd with the summer light,
The full-juiced apple, waxing over-mellow,
Drops in a silent autumn night.
All its allotted length of days
The flower ripens in its place,
Ripens and fades, and falls, and hath no toil,
Fast-rooted in the fruitful soil.

IV

Hateful is the dark-blue sky,
Vaulted o'er the dark-blue sea.
Death is the end of life; ah, why
Should life all labour be?
Let us alone. Time driveth onward fast,
And in a little while our lips are dumb.
Let us alone. What is it that will last?
All things are taken from us, and become
Portions and parcels of the dreadful past.
Let us alone. What pleasure can we have
To war with evil? Is there any peace
In ever climbing up the climbing wave?
All things have rest, and ripen toward the grave
In silence; ripen, fall and cease:
Give us long rest or death, dark death, or dreamful ease.

V

How sweet it were, hearing the downward stream,
With half-shut eyes ever to seem
Falling asleep in a half-dream!
To dream and dream, like yonder amber light,
Which will not leave the myrrh-bush on the height;
To hear each other's whisper'd speech;
Eating the Lotos day by day,
To watch the crisping ripples on the beach,
And tender curving lines of creamy spray;
To lend our hearts and spirits wholly
To the influence of mild-minded melancholy;
To muse and brood and live again in memory,
With those old faces of our infancy
Heap'd over with a mound of grass,
Two handfuls of white dust, shut in an urn of brass!

VI

Dear is the memory of our wedded lives,
And dear the last embraces of our wives
And their warm tears: but all hath suffer'd change:
For surely now our household hearths are cold,
Our sons inherit us: our looks are strange:
And we should come like ghosts to trouble joy.
Or else the island princes over-bold
Have eat our substance, and the minstrel sings
Before them of the ten years' war in Troy,
And our great deeds, as half-forgotten things.
Is there confusion in the little isle?
Let what is broken so remain.
The Gods are hard to reconcile:
'Tis hard to settle order once again.
There is confusion worse than death,
Trouble on trouble, pain on pain,
Long labour unto aged breath,
Sore task to hearts worn out by many wars
And eyes grown dim with gazing on the pilot-stars.

VII

But, propt on beds of amaranth and moly,
How sweet (while warm airs lull us, blowing lowly)
With half-dropt eyelid still,
Beneath a heaven dark and holy,
To watch the long bright river drawing slowly
His waters from the purple hill--
To hear the dewy echoes calling
From cave to cave thro' the thick-twined vine--
To watch the emerald-colour'd water falling
Thro' many a wov'n acanthus-wreath divine!
Only to hear and see the far-off sparkling brine,
Only to hear were sweet, stretch'd out beneath the pine.

VIII

The Lotos blooms below the barren peak:
The Lotos blows by every winding creek:
All day the wind breathes low with mellower tone:
Thro' every hollow cave and alley lone
Round and round the spicy downs the yellow Lotos-dust is blown.
We have had enough of action, and of motion we,
Roll'd to starboard, roll'd to larboard, when the surge was seething free,
Where the wallowing monster spouted his foam-fountains in the sea.
Let us swear an oath, and keep it with an equal mind,
In the hollow Lotos-land to live and lie reclined
On the hills like Gods together, careless of mankind.
For they lie beside their nectar, and the bolts are hurl'd
Far below them in the valleys, and the clouds are lightly curl'd
Round their golden houses, girdled with the gleaming world:
Where they smile in secret, looking over wasted lands,
Blight and famine, plague and earthquake, roaring deeps and fiery sands,
Clanging fights, and flaming towns, and sinking ships, and praying hands.
But they smile, they find a music centred in a doleful song
Steaming up, a lamentation and an ancient tale of wrong,
Like a tale of little meaning tho' the words are strong;
Chanted from an ill-used race of men that cleave the soil,
Sow the seed, and reap the harvest with enduring toil,
Storing yearly little dues of wheat, and wine and oil;
Till they perish and they suffer--some, 'tis whisper'd--down in hell
Suffer endless anguish, others in Elysian valleys dwell,
Resting weary limbs at last on beds of asphodel.
Surely, surely, slumber is more sweet than toil, the shore
Than labour in the deep mid-ocean, wind and wave and oar;
O, rest ye, brother mariners, we will not wander more.